Women Starting Over and Moving Up

Building Financial Success On Your Own Terms

The Honorable Nora Ellen

Women Starting Over and Moving Up: Building Financial Success On Your Own Terms

www.WomenMovingUp.com

Copyright © 2021 Nora Ellen

ISBN: 979-8749956207

All rights reserved. No portion of this book may be reproduced mechanically, electronically, or by any other means, including photocopying, without permission of the publisher or author except in the case of brief quotations embodied in critical articles and reviews. It is illegal to copy this book, post it to a website, or distribute it by any other means without permission from the publisher or author.

References to internet websites (URLs) were accurate at the time of writing. Authors and the publishers are not responsible for URLs that may have expired or changed since the manuscript was prepared.

Limits of Liability and Disclaimer of Warranty

The author and publisher shall not be liable for your misuse of the enclosed material. This book is strictly for informational and educational purposes only.

Warning – Disclaimer

The purpose of this book is to educate and entertain. The author and/or publisher do not guarantee that anyone following these techniques, suggestions, tips, ideas, or strategies will become successful. The author and/or publisher shall have neither liability nor responsibility to anyone with respect to any loss or damage caused, or alleged to be caused, directly or indirectly by the information contained in this book.

Medical Disclaimer

The medical or health information in this book is provided as an information resource only, and is not to be used or relied on for any diagnostic or treatment purposes. This information is not intended to be patient education, does not create any patient-physician relationship, and should not be used as a substitute for professional diagnosis and treatment.

Publisher
10-10-10 Publishing
Markham, ON
Canada

Printed in the United States and Canada

Dedication

This book is lovingly dedicated to my precious granddaughters: Liana, Calielle, Hazel, Brinley and Baby Girl Mesnard. Remember, it costs nothing to dream big—but everything if you don't. With God, all things are possible.

Table of Contents

Foreword ix

How to Read This Book xi

Chapter 1 – What Ever Happened to My Dream Life? 1
    From Broke to Hope to Success 3
    "Starting Over" Tools for Success 10
    Don't Be Trapped by Your Thoughts 11
    I Did It; You Can Do It 15
    Fun Exercise 17

Chapter 2 – Yes, You Can Start Over 19
    Say Goodbye to the Old to Make Way for the New 21
    How to Renew, Refresh, Reset 24
    Fun Exercise 31
    Success Story from Jeremee Quijada to Nora Ellen 32

Chapter 3 – Preparing for Your New Journey 33
    Preparing Is Taking the Right Action 34
    Make it About the Journey and Not the End 35
    Letting Go 37
    Burying the Hatchet, Which Really Means to Forgive 38

Self-Care for a Healthy You 41

Create Your Very Own Starting Over Plan 44

Fun Exercise 46

Chapter 4 – You Have the Power to Take Control of Your Life 47

The Power of Thought 48

Your Power Is Within, Not Outside Yourself 50

Unbottle the Emotions 51

Dump Those Self-Limiting Beliefs 52

Rethink Comfort 54

Simplify Your Health With Choices 55

Your Thought Treasure Chest 57

Fear Forward 59

Dump the Imposter Syndrome 60

Manage Your Expectations 61

Focus Your Mind 62

Reward Yourself 63

Live Loved, Love Yourself 64

Chapter 5 – Becoming Someone Else 67

Habits—What to Have and What to Discard 68

The Power of "I Am" 70

Leveraging the Power of Affirmations 70

Define Your Big Why 72

Have a Greater Purpose 74

- Draw up a Dream List 75
- Believing in Your Self-Worth 79
- Success Story from Kim Mladenov to Nora Ellen 80

Chapter 6 – The 9 Pinnacles of Power 81
- Power of Clarity 81
- Power of Proximity 82
- Power of Purity 83
- Power of Enthusiasm 85
- Power of Determination 88
- Power of Authority 90
- Power of Humor 92
- Power of Joy 94
- Power of Love 96
- Fun Exercise 97

Chapter 7 – The Help You Don't Know You Have 99
- Where Do You Start? 100
- Help Is on the Other Side of a Relationship 101
- Connecting and Networking 102
- In a Season of Growth, Give to Others 105
- Big Changes Start with Small Steps 106

Chapter 8 – Awaken the Leader in You 113
- Success Story from Mary Ann S. Chavez to
Nora Ellen 133

Chapter 9 – The 8 Characteristics of Success 135

    Characteristic #1 – Bravery 136

    Characteristic #2 – An Upbeat Attitude 137

    Characteristic #3 – Integrity 139

    Characteristic #4 – Trustworthiness 140

    Characteristic #5 – Persistence 142

    Characteristic #6 – A Mindset for Hard Work 144

    Characteristic #7 – Maintain Vitality 145

    Characteristic #8 – Be an Expert in at Least One Area 147

Chapter 10 – Negotiate Your Monetary Worth and Promotion 151

    What If You Were Overlooked 153

    The Day of the Meeting 156

    Negotiating the Best Terms on a Job Offer 160

    Some Tips to Negotiate New Contracts with New Clients 162

    New to the Workforce 163

Chapter 11 – You Are the CEO of Your Life 165

    What are Legacy Entrepreneurs? 167

    Becoming an Entrepreneur 168

Foreword

Having to start over is scary, especially if you are a woman. As a woman, you have a lot going against you in the workplace, especially when you choose to reinvent yourself. But let me assure you it's not all downhill from here. In fact, this may be the best time of your life because you are the one in charge, not anyone else.

Sometimes, you are forced to do over because of external factors, such as being laid off or your business had to shut down, or you're being sidelined by ageism or technology. Or you are broke because your marriage suddenly ended and having been a stay-at-home mom for years has not given you any skills to join the workforce with. On the other hand, maybe, you are deliberately choosing to start over because you want to follow your passion, or you are determined to ask for what you are truly worth.

Transitioning to a new job or a new promotion is often perceived to be hard. But it's difficult mainly because you are in the dark as to how to make it happen.

That is why Nora Ellen's book *Women Starting Over and Moving Up: Building Financial Success on Your Own Terms* is so refreshing and very important for the times we are living in. Nora has dug deep into her own life and her own career do-overs in the first instance, because she became a single mom with two kids after a divorce, and in the second, because she was suddenly left out in the cold after being divorced by her second husband. Nora had to start over twice.

It's from this perspective that Nora gives you the necessary principles and practical tools you need to overcome the inevitable challenges. Plus, she sprinkles throughout the book fun tips and exercises to help you cut through the doubt, obstacles and frustrations that will crop up. What I especially appreciate is that if there is an overriding theme that runs throughout this book, it's Nora's advice to you to choose faith over fear and to choose living over regret.

So, what exactly can you expect to learn from these pages?

- Master your own thoughts to redesign your future
- Maximize your options by finding your own community and creating a Mastermind Group
- Leverage the 9 Pinnacles of Power to create positive outcomes
- Reinvent yourself while balancing financial success and emotional satisfaction
- Start over or move up on your terms; know that the time is right when you choose to

I encourage you to read this book a chapter at a time, and to take the prescribed steps as soon as you can. Nora has provided you with the tools and ideas that have the potential to powerfully change and remake your life. It's up to you to act on them to get to the financial success and the fulfilling life you have dreamed of and so richly deserve.

Loral Langemeier
The Millionaire Maker

How to Read This Book

Why would you need a primer to read this book?

My answer to that is, as young kids, we were sent to school to learn without first being taught how to learn. We were just expected, as little children, to instinctively know how to learn. It was this way for me in school; I was never taught how to learn or take good notes in a class. When I got to college, I took a Western Civilization course, where I took a lot of good notes. Or so I thought. I wrote down everything that I thought was important, from what the professor said. I did not do well in that class and had to take it over again, since my notes were wrong. I decided to borrow the notes of an 'A' student the next time I took the class. You can imagine, I did a lot better. Why didn't I know to write down what she did? I was never taught that skill. Thus, this book is written in a way you can easily understand.

This is not your typical book, but it's exactly the book you need for this time in your life. It's filled with timeless principles. It is not for the faint of heart; it's not filled with lighthearted frippery that doesn't get you to the place of strength during this particular season of your life. I cover tough subjects, and you will most likely feel uncomfortable with what I share and suggest, but straight talk is necessary for your success.

The reason I am giving you this heads-up is because of my own personal experience. I have read and enjoyed many books about a person who reached financial success. But when I got to the part where I had to do the exercises that would push me into a new way of thinking, I quit reading. I didn't understand my aversion until later in my life. Growing and learning is work, and it takes focus and concentration. Learning to think in a newer, better way is uncomfortable. But if you are desiring to do better in your life and achieve more, and are ready for it, you can push through being uncomfortable. There are questions to ask yourself in some of the chapters. Get a special notebook to write down your answers; this will help you grow faster and in a more carefree way. You'll love the new you that you will become as you look back at your answers. Being broke is hard; success is hard. Pick your hard.

My disclaimer: Don't believe a word I say here. Research for yourself what I have written in this book. We have our different religious beliefs, different political beliefs, different upbringings and cultural backgrounds—different this, different that. Take what you need of my story, perspectives, and experiences that you can use. There is a lot here to help you start over and over again and move up to get to the wealth and financial success you desire. Now is your chance to start over and leave a lasting legacy!

Starting over is an adventure. If I can do it, so can you. Here we go!

Chapter 1

What Ever Happened to My Dream Life?

"Don't be afraid to start over. It's a brand new opportunity to rebuild what you truly want."
—Andre Pascal

A string of traumatic setbacks—divorce, financial distress, broken dreams, becoming a single mom without a way of making money—was never part of my dream life. But my life did not turn out the way I expected. I was brought up in Colorado to be a wife, a mother, and to be of service to our community, because that was what my mom did and what our family valued.

So I was not prepared for two broken marriages, ending up as a single mom, and having to start over financially by myself to put food on the table for me and my two young children. But I did, and successfully too, on both occasions. The first reset was by necessity, as well as the second one. This one I am journeying through right now, is by choice. The first time I started over was driven by the need to survive and to make sure I had some financial security, and that I was not letting my kids down, as a single mother.

This time around, I am starting over myself because I am fueled by a purpose and a plan to help other women who may be walking in my old shoes. I am driven by a commitment to help as many women as I can, who may feel disempowered by money and income, and to give hope and to positively impact lives around the world.

Too often, women find themselves at the short end of the stick when their world comes crashing down in a matter of seconds. It could be any number of unfortunate and ugly events: faced with divorce, being widowed, out of a job, burdened by failed businesses, stuck with skills made obsolete by technology, facing gender discrimination or ageism.

What do you do when your boat is rocked so badly and so unexpectedly, and you are out of money, out of ideas, and out of options? Where do you go when that happens? How do you start over? Where do you go next? Who do you turn to?

I can help you get from where you are now, to where you want to be. I have been in this place before, where you are now, and I am fueled by a plan and a purpose to reach out and uplift women who need help starting over: to share with you my experiences so you can have hope, and to offer you an inspirational example to follow to avoid making mistakes; to elevate you with stories of other women who have come this way before and have achieved the success they have only dreamed of; to guide you in starting over, because you'll be starting with a clean slate.

Why do I want to do this?

Because women deserve better.

You deserve better.

Because women are powerhouses.

You are smart, entrepreneurial, family-oriented, caring, compassionate, and creative.

Because women are leaders, savers, creators, keepers of societies, business geniuses.

You have untapped power within you.

Because by giving women more income-earning opportunities, they invest back into families and communities.

You just have to own it.

Here is my disclaimer: This is not to say men don't need help starting over. I totally value men and the contributions they have made to our world, but in this instance, I am writing this book for women.

From Broke to Hope to Success

I never graduated from college. I did attend for 4 years to become a teacher, because I wanted to positively impact young lives, as my teachers did mine. I actually wanted to be a Physical Education teacher because, growing up, students always looked up to the PE teachers, and they greatly influenced the lives of their students. However, there was something fundamental I wanted to change.

When it came to divvying up the class into teams for sports, the PE teacher tended to rely on a popular student or the sports jock to select the students. I would always watch as the team leaders bandied back and forth on whom they wanted on their respective teams. Their top picks would be the star athletes, followed by those students with okay abilities, like me. Finally, the last group would be made of those students who were unfit, overweight, too uncoordinated, too short, too unpopular.

Did this happen in your school? Is this a memory you can relate to? I always felt so badly for the last group because they were always made to feel that they were the least of the crop. School was supposed to be an environment set up to motivate students to rise to their highest potential; instead, the least sporty among us ended up being humiliated. Watching this unfold time and time again, I resolved that I would be a PE teacher, and I would teach class in such a way that every student would feel welcomed, important, and worthy.

I first went to study at Covenant College, on Lookout Mountain, Tennessee, and then to the University of Northern Colorado, which was one of the top three in the nation for teachers. However, despite the four years of study, I didn't finish college, because I chose to get married. My then fiancé was going into the military, and we would be frequently transferred around the country. I thought I would finish my education later, but that didn't happen; we moved around a lot and I had two children. I sold some Avon products, and volunteered in community and church groups, but that summed up my work experience.

After getting divorced, I moved back home, and I prayed and asked God to help me get a good job and take care of myself and my children. I saw a great job posting and applied. I did not get the job and was so disappointed. But, knowing God and His goodness, I applied for another job and did get that job quickly. It was better than the first one I applied for. It was better pay and I had my own office looking out over the beautiful Front

Range mountains. I was even able to move into my own place. Somehow, along the way, I discovered I was quite good at acing job interviews, so I ended up in higher-level jobs that I wasn't qualified for. I believed if a company didn't hire me, there would be another job somewhere.

I was 28 when my first marriage fell apart. I was no longer able to handle my husband's anger. I remarried on the rebound, just one year after my divorce. I didn't take the time to recover from my first broken marriage, but after 18 years, and when the cracks in my second marriage became irreparable fissures, I came to grips with the realization that I had regarding having a man in my life as the solution to all my financial and other problems, and the key to my happiness. I also had made a man my financial plan and had believed that a man would rescue me. I did whatever I could to save the marriage, but my second husband didn't want to go along with me. I was willing to make changes, but he blamed the faults in our marriage entirely on me. It was when I went to counseling and recovery, after my second divorce, that this truth—that I looked to a man to make me happy and to save me—crystallized, because I had to look within myself as to why I ended up in two failed marriages. Along the way, I discovered the healing and changes I needed to make within myself, with God's help.

After my second divorce, I was without a job. I had been a homemaker all these years, and there was no clear way for me to find work, but there was pressure on me to make money to take care of myself and my children. I knew I had to do something and, in examining my options, I came to realize that I didn't want to work for someone, nor for a company. I did not want to go get a job, any job, like most people do.

After praying for more guidance, once again an idea sprang to mind. I had heard about people that were earning good money "flipping" houses, and decided to explore this further by reading books and joining a local real estate investors group. In those days, the Internet was not nearly as sophisticated or as easily accessible as it is now, where we can learn new things, join meet-up groups, download apps and, in general, get information in seconds, or at the very least, in minutes.

Nonetheless, being in groups of like-minded people who were involved in what I wanted to learn about, was highly motivating, and it spurred me to take action.

> **Here's a tip:** One of the best ways to be successful is to find like-minded people who are already successful at what you want to achieve.

Armed with new knowledge and purpose, I set out to find houses that I could renovate a little and flip, or do a lease option (like rent-to-own). This was the time (in 2003/2004) before the subprime loan crisis blew up, and I was qualified to buy a house using what was called a "no-doc" loan, which was a loan that didn't require any income documentation on my part. I could also access what were called "hard money loans," where a borrower could get a short-term loan at a very high rate of interest, with the house being provided as collateral.

So, I found my first house from a yard sign on the road. The owner, Jim, was from Nebraska, and somehow that made me believe that he would stand by his word on the price and terms we agreed to. In short, I bought the house on a handshake. However, the deal fell through soon enough. Jim called to say he just couldn't get himself to sell his house then. He explained that he might reconsider his decision later, just not at that point in time. I was stuck—my first transaction was a bust. But I wasn't going to let that deter me. And here's another tip: You are bound to make mistakes, especially at the start of any new ventures, but don't give up. Put it down to a learning opportunity.

I changed my strategy. I decided to buy my next house at an auction, as the prices would be significantly below market. I did my homework and settled for a relatively new home, which only needed some light cosmetic work to give it a facelift. Arizona is what you would call a trustee state, and real estate auctions are carried out on the Arizona Court House steps, and they can be dominated by a few investment bidders. I knew of one such company from the real estate investment group I had joined, and decided to pay a bidding company to represent me.

Unexpectedly, Jim came back, ready to sell his place. Thus, I ended up with two investment houses, both bringing in a good amount of cash flow. I also decided to create different sales pricing strategies for the two houses I now owned. For the first one, I created a lease option, where the actual price of the house was fixed for when the buyer was able to make the purchase. I did not put a sales price ceiling on the second house, and I was very fortunate with my timing. This was the time when real estate prices were escalating, with no stops in sight. I made $11,000 on Jim's house, and was blessed enough to make tens of thousands of dollars on the second house that I bought at the auction. I figured rightly in my timing, in getting in at a good time and selling before the bubble burst in 2008, when the subprime loan crisis exploded. With the club I joined and the books I read, along with good timing, I was able to make the money I needed in a little over a year.

With real estate prices storming ahead into what seemed to be bubble territory, flipping houses no longer seemed like a wise option for me. Now I had to start over financially, yet again. I realized that I had to make money in a more sustainable and different way in my third time starting over. I prayed for guidance on what to do. At the advice of a good male friend, I hired a career coach named George, for $150. It was the best investment in myself that I had ever made.

George was inspiring and uplifting. He reframed how I viewed myself, and showed me that I had many more marketable skills and abilities than I had thought I possessed. He gave me a new way to take inventory of my skills, my gifts, talents, my volunteer work, limited work experience, and knowledge base. He helped me update my very old resume, and placed me in his mastermind group with his other clients so we could exchange ideas, encourage each other, and network to find work. It is vitally important, when you are starting over, to surround yourself with solid support such as a mastermind group. This is a topic I shall cover more fully in Chapter 6.

In a conversation with a gentleman in the mastermind group, we explored what it was I had done, was interested in, and had grown up with. I mentioned that my dad was in real estate: He had his own firm and had completed a few developments. As a youth, I went to his office to help him out, and I also loved to hang around him when he was on the phone handling his real estate and development deals. This was well before the age of call waiting, and the children were warned off the phone when Dad was expecting a business call.

This particular conversation prompted a line of questioning, something you need to ask of yourself when you are taking inventory of yourself when starting over:

- What have I done?
- What am I familiar with?
- What skills do I have?
- What talents do I have?
- Where have I been successful?
- What do I enjoy?
- What do others say I am good at?

Based on that line of questioning, I decided to get my license to sell real estate. That got me started on a career that has lasted for over 12 years, during which I made a six-figure income. But I felt I was bumping against a ceiling. My earnings as a real estate agent never went much above $150,000. When I dug deep into myself to redefine myself yet again, I realized that I had an inner money thermostat that was subconsciously influencing me, which set a limit on how much money I earned. I found that growing up, phrases like "filthy money" would be bandied around, and somehow the concepts like "money doesn't grow on trees" and "tainted wealth" had permeated my subconscious and put brakes on my earnings potential.

I have, on many occasions, felt guilt over money. We have often heard, "Money is the root of all evil," but this is actually misquoted from a verse in the Bible and taken completely out of context. The verse really says, *For the LOVE of money is A root of all KINDS of evil for which some have strayed from the faith in their greediness and pierced themselves through with many sorrows* (1 Timothy 6:10). We can all agree that if money is sought after for selfish gain, rather than how it can help, then it can lead us down a dangerous path, which is what that verse is about. We know that the love of money is not the root of evil acts such as rape or dissipation, but it can be the root of crimes like murder or theft. Such kinds of misinterpretations, misperceptions and misunderstandings can hamstring us in life by creating dysfunctional attitudes toward money. I know it did for me. Does it sound like a defective money thermostat might be part of your story?

How to hack and improve your inner money thermostat is one of the tips you will get in my webinars, coaching, trainings, and online courses that you can find on my website, www.WomenMovingUp.com shown at the top of the page. It's very crucial to dismantle that programming if you want to achieve success. Otherwise, you may find yourself with some modicum of success, but you'll be frustrated for not exceeding the upper limits of your money thermostat, and for letting your full potential waste away.

"Starting Over" Tools for Success

As part of my financial coaching, I created a podcast—"Women Starting Over"—to inspire, motivate, and energize women to get the income and financial success they long to have. Whether you are facing job obsolescence, insufficient retirement savings, bankruptcy, or even eviction, you CAN elevate yourself to build new habits of thinking and wealth that will bring you lasting satisfaction and financial freedom.

In my preparation for writing this book, I set out to interview women who had to start over and who have since become very successful. Did they have traits in common? What drove them to stand in the face of loss and come out stronger as winners?

Among these fabulous women are Stella, a lovely African American, who ended up as a young single mom and then started over with just a pencil and paper. Now she is the writer of school curriculum, a real estate investor, and the author of a dozen books. Another is Neece, the first generation of immigrants from the Philippines, who ended up on welfare when she became pregnant in college. She is now enjoying a successful career and is helping give foster kids a loving home. Still another is Aleta, who surprisingly ended up divorced with no career, but now has a very successful network marketing business in health and wellness. (See the link at the top of the book pages for the website to listen to their courageous stories or read about in my blog.)

Don't Be Trapped by Your Thoughts

When you are attempting to repair your life from a severe setback, it is almost inevitable that your self-confidence is eroded to an all-time low. As you read this book, and when you listen to my podcast, you may find yourself saying, "I can't do that," or "I don't have those kinds of options where I live," or "I'm not good enough, I'm not as strong as these women, I'm not as qualified," or "I'm a failure."

Let me assure you that all of these statements are far from the truth. They may reflect how you are feeling now, but you have within you the assets and the resources you need in order to turn your life around. Your mind is your best asset. It can also be your worst asset if you get drowned in self-limiting beliefs, so the key to renewing yourself and resetting your life is to change how you think, or more importantly, how you CHOOSE to think and believe.

Many of us fall into the trap of thinking that we will be better off when our current circumstances or environment changes. We tell ourselves that we will feel more at peace and we'll be happier if our outer situation is improved or changed. Alas, this line of thinking is intrinsic in the American culture, which suggests, through movies, television, advertising, and even social media, that being thinner, having a new car, a new dress or a man, will make us happier.

In truth, it really is the other way around. It's our inner life that will impact us the most, because it's what's taking place on the inside that creates what is happening to us on the outside. And our inner life is absolutely within our control. If there is one thing you want to take away from this chapter, take this: How you feel is not who you are. How you feel—your emotions—are triggered by how and what you think. When something happens to you, your first response is your thought, followed by the emotion that is spurred by your thought.

Let's take as an example my first real estate deal with Jim. I was still a newbie in flipping houses, and purchasing his house would have been my very first transaction. When he called to cancel the sale, my first reaction could have been, "This is a bad start; I'll never make it," and I could have felt despondent or disheartened. If I had let those emotions get the better of me, they might even have derailed my new start in real estate investing. But instead, I shrugged off the disappointment and changed my strategy.

Without understanding that the thought is the precursor to the emotion, you fall into the trap of reacting to what's around you or what happens to you. You become reactive as opposed to being thoughtfully responsive. It might be far easier if you viewed your emotion as an indicator or a piece of information that gives you more understanding about yourself. When an emotion bubbles up, be it feeling overwhelmed, guilty, or unwanted, accept that emotion. But don't become attached to it and have it become a truth in your life.

Thoughts are things. They lead to all kinds of emotions, but also to all kinds of beautiful and savvy inventions, art, and music. The lovely things you are surrounded by—the products and technology that make your life so much easier than those of your grandparents—were firstly just thoughts in the minds of people, who then followed through with them.

By themselves, some thoughts are not good or bad. It is the heart behind the thoughts, how we process them, and the actions we take from our thoughts, that is important to consider. Understand that thoughts are sometimes neutral and come to life with the meaning we give to them. What has happened to you takes as much weight as the meaning you give to the story. When you intentionally choose to only think those thoughts that support you and others, you change how you feel, and just as importantly, you will get rid of the triggers that made you upset or angry. You reap enormous benefits when you consciously control your thoughts, rather than being controlled by your thoughts. When you are able to think clearly and deliberately, you are more able to identify and see the opportunities that lie ahead of you.

You can control your thoughts, and when you do so, you take back control of how you feel. You don't have to believe any of your thoughts. Choose instead to master your mind and choose power thinking. T. Harv Eker, the author of *Secrets of the Millionaire Mind: Mastering the Inner Game of Wealth*, defines power thinking as deliberately choosing those thoughts that support you and your success. It takes a while to get good at power thinking. It's similar to learning a new skill. You need to keep at it and develop it as a habit, and you will get good at it.

T. Harv Eker summarized it this way in his best-selling book: "Thoughts lead to feelings, which lead to actions, which lead to results."

Thoughts → Feelings → Actions → Results

Be clear about the results and outcomes you want to have!

It's crucial to understand that the obstacles and upsets you are going through are not meant to punish you. In fact, they are meant to stir you to greatness.

I believe our Creator lovingly allows a shaking in our lives so we can awaken to new beginnings by shedding off old ways that limit us.

You may find it hard to fathom those words when your days are filled with pain, help is nowhere to be found, and any faith you may have in anyone or anything has been shredded to bits.

Let's try this. Ask yourself this question: What if all that you are going through, or have gone through, is meant to get you to rise up in courage—to *step up* and to *elevate* to your own, true potential; to get you to *claim* your own great successes—and to understand that women starting over are not starting with nothing to their name, but are starting with guts, wisdom, and learned experiences earned the hard way?

I Did It; You Can Do It

You can put the painful past behind.

I've done it; many others before us have done it.

You can do it too.

I won't say it will be easy, especially in the beginning.

Putting the past behind is never easy.

You may be racked with guilt. You'll be in anguish when you realize that this—a failed marriage, a non-starter career, or an empty bank account—is what has become of your dream life.

But do you know what the good news is?

The future is yours for the taking.

It is yours to remake and to reimagine as you want it to be.

Intentionally live with purpose, and discover your destiny.

Make it big, make it fierce, and make it yours.

Rewards await you.

Build it exciting, add fun into it, inject ease and comfort, and include friendship and partnership and community.

And you won't be doing it alone.

I am right here, helping you take the necessary steps, some easier than others.

I will help you start over with clarity, confidence, and a spring in your step.

And when your conviction cracks, and you lose a little faith, I will hold your hand until you regain your poise and step forward with belief and trust . . . in yourself.

I write this book for all women needing help to forge a new future. But as a single mom myself, I lean toward single mothers who have to slog it alone. Single moms face different challenges: They have to be a parent, homemaker, breadwinner, and be all things that their kids need. Many single moms shove aside their own desires and needs for the sake of their children.

But there is also another special group I hope would benefit greatly from this book. These are women who are victims of domestic violence.

I am writing this book during the unprecedented Covid-19 pandemic, in 2021, and sadly, one of the many unreported statistics, buried among Covid-19 daily infection and death figures, is the markedly increasing numbers of cases of domestic violence around the world, as vulnerable women are stuck at home in the pandemic response, with their abusers.

The pandemic has exacerbated what has existed for a very long time. Women have been victims of domestic violence or "intimate violence"; but pre-pandemic, there were avenues for women to escape. When they mustered enough strength and courage, they could escape to rebuild their broken lives and create a future for themselves, where they can be successful, live out creative and fulfilling lives, and take charge of their own futures.

I know abuse is abuse; it hurts regardless of whether it is physical or psychological.

Both are equally damaging. I want to show women that even if they are scarred physically or psychologically, they have within themselves the reserves of courage to get help, hit the reset button and, yes, to start over.

Fun Exercise

When you are starting over, everything can feel confusing and overwhelming: What do you do, where do you go, and what are your next steps?

Scattered throughout the book are fun exercises to help you dismantle old habits, build new ones, and to clarify your path forward. This one helped to center me considerably by grounding me and helping me narrow down what I wanted to avoid and what I really desired to be engaged in when starting over.

1. Take two differently colored pieces of paper; for example, one pink and one green, or whatever are your favorites or you have at hand.

2. Place them on the refrigerator or somewhere you spend a lot of time during the day. It could be on a board in your home office.

3. When you think of something wonderful or something that moves your heart, write that down on one of these

papers. It could be a new client, a sparkling gem, a phone call from an old friend, or anything that brings a smile to your face.

4. On the other piece of paper, jot down what upsets you, what you dislike, or what you would want to change in your world.

5. Make it a fun, creative exercise by using different colors of marker pens or pencils. You can add doodles or little sketches that express how you are feeling during those moments you are making your list.

At the end of a week or so, look over your lists and summarize the important points. Do this a few times or as often as you need, till you are clear on identifying what will help in moving your new path forward.

Chapter 2

Yes, You Can Start Over

*"Life isn't about finding yourself.
Life is about creating yourself."*
—George Bernard Shaw

There is a truth I would like to establish from the get go.

Starting over doesn't mean giving up.

Starting over means creating a new beginning.

But before we go any further into how to build a new future with ease, let's answer the question of why you would choose to start over. Why would anyone leave all that is familiar behind? Starting over is a highly personal decision, made for any number of reasons. You can do so by choice to:

- Move ahead to a higher-paying job with responsibilities that are a match to your skills.
- Leave a soul-crushing corporate job for something more meaningful and purposeful.

- Make your own needs more of a priority.
- Develop a new business idea that offers a service to unmet needs.
- Launch a product idea in the market.

When you start over, one question keeps cropping up. It may throw you into confusion at first, and you may get frustrated when you don't get immediate answers. However, look at the question as the key to creating your new beginning; and when you do, you've taken the first step on this journey.

"What do you want?" This is the question that will hound you and irritate you. When I was forming my own starting over journey, and was attending motivational seminars with leaders like Bob Proctor, this was the question he asked repeatedly in his seminars. When I first heard this question, it made me squirm and feel uncomfortable. He asked it so often that he nudged me into thinking about my life and giving myself the permission to think of what I want. To many of you who have always put the needs of others before your own, thinking about what you want can seem kind of selfish, unspiritual and an exercise in self-centeredness and self-absorption.

Let me say, that attitude is wrong. If you don't know what you want, where you end up will be chosen for you by others. By not thinking through this important process, you are yielding control of your life to external factors, be they people or circumstances. A vague concept of wanting more money, or willingly drifting through life because you are unwilling to answer this question, will not get you the kind of financial success you are seeking.

We will discuss this important knowledge in more detail later—I won't let you wriggle out of this like I used to try to do.

Say Goodbye to the Old to Make Way for the New

Stepping onto a new path, one you've never tried before, can be scary. But there are ways to make it easier on yourself, and that is to lighten the load by junking the energetic baggage of the past.

What are some of the pieces you need to disown?

- **Fear:** Fear can be overwhelming. I am sure you may be feeling scared if you have to start over, or scared and excited if you are choosing to. Fear is just a feeling and an emotion, and can feel overwhelmingly strong during those times when you are unsure of your next steps; but know that you are not alone. Our Creator made sure you were born with gifts, talents, and a great personality and a good brain that can learn and relearn what you need to know to start over and succeed. I have heard this said: *F.E.A.R. is False Evidence Appearing Real.* A recent study[1] of people with Generalized Anxiety Disorder (GAD) showed that 91% of what they feared did not materialize. One way to defuse nameless fear is to get closer to your faith or belief system, which will lend strength to you during this time in your life. There is good fear, the kind that motivates us to act, and the insidious fear of the worst that could possibly happen.

---

1 Lucas S. LaFreniere, Michelle G. Newman, Exposing Worry's Deceit: Percentage of Untrue Worries in Generalized Anxiety Disorder Treatment, Behavior Therapy, Elsevier, May 2020

But in reality, our worst fears rarely materialize. Fear in small doses can be a helpful friend, but having too much of it turns into a damaging enemy emotionally, mentally, and physically. Understand that we all live with a certain level of uncertainty, because life would be very boring if we knew ahead of time everything that would take place or happen.

- **Guilt:** Beating yourself up is an affliction common to many women wanting to start over. You feel guilty that you didn't do enough, and therefore you have to start over. Starting over doesn't mean you failed. One of the world's greatest inventors, Thomas Edison, said he failed all the way to success. Don't feel guilty about wanting a redo. It means that you have made a choice to do something different, something more rewarding, more aligned with your passion, and more personally rewarding.

- **Regret:** It looks like guilt, but it doesn't feel the same. Regret is looking back at the turns you didn't take on your old road, and worrying or fantasizing about how your life would have been different had you taken a different fork in the road. Maybe you regret not finishing high school or college; perhaps you feel remorse over not trying harder for a promotion. Regret takes the form of a series of "what if" questions, to which you have no answers because all that has happened in the past is no longer relevant. What got you to this exact point in time, what happened to you in your past, is not who you are now or desire to be. That was then; this is now. You can live in this new now.

- **Doubt and Lack of Belief:** These are also "feeling" states and emotions that can severely hinder you. Your desire to need to start over may have been prompted by a financial loss or a severe downturn in your investments. But losses like that can cut very deeply and seep into various parts of your life. You may feel a loss of self-confidence or self-belief because you lost your job, and you may doubt your own abilities. And you get discouraged, which in turn saps your energy and motivation to create a new and different future for yourself.

- **Playing the Victim:** I know the phrase sounds harsh, but you're not reading this book to be coddled, and I'm not going to skip over what can hinder you. I used to be a blamer; it's easy to blame others or complain about how life's unfair because you're being forced to start over. It's easy to latch onto excuses or replay injustices that you feel were doled out to you, and to play the victim. For a while, it may work to get others to sympathize with you and cut you favors because they feel sorry for you. But playing the victim and blaming others held me back, and it can only hold you back too. It's time to stop seeing yourself this way. It's time to believe you're no longer a victim, and view yourself through the fresh lens of a new beginning.

- **Stuck in the Past:** When the going gets uncomfortable, the past and the familiar may feel very good to you, and you long to rewind the clock. Don't cling to the familiar, or relish the good old days, especially when the going gets uncomfortable. Anything new will feel uncomfortable, like new shoes that may pinch. But that feeling is temporary.

- **Dysfunctional Habits:** Ask yourself what no longer serves you. What beliefs are impeding your progress forward? What habits do you need to break that no longer serve you? Are they procrastination, over-analyzing, or needing to control everything? Whatever they are, be aware of them to know what to change.

How to Renew, Refresh, Reset

A journey of a thousand miles begins with a single step. Don't wait to take the first step, because if you do, you'll be standing in the same place a year or two years from now. Be willing to ask the right questions, and be brave enough to alter the trajectory of your path forward when new answers appear. Don't get distracted by pointless details or over-worrying.

I will confess that right at the beginning, the concept of starting over felt like a huge stretch I didn't want to take. I saw that it would take the kind of thinking, processing, wondering and dreaming I wasn't used to. I had to force myself to go through these steps. It was uncomfortable. I felt selfish, because by questioning and daydreaming, it felt like I didn't trust God. Then I pondered on my choices. Was I limiting myself by letting my alternatives be shaped by what I knew already existed in the marketplace? Were there opportunities I was unaware of? Where do I look to even know and define what I want? There is the wanting of better character and the wanting of material things . . . so many different kinds of wanting.

I journaled a lot on who I wanted to be. What do I want to be known for, remembered for, and sought after for? It took a lot of practice but I persisted. During this time, someone posed a question I very much appreciated: "If money or time wasn't an issue, what would you do, be, or want?" That question got me thinking and excited, as if I was finally given permission to fly high with my dreams. I understood that what I immediately came up with, need not be right or wrong, or permanently etched as my goals. It helped to know that my motives were right. The more successful I become, the more people I can help in keeping with one of my core beliefs, which is that life is about loving God and people, and helping others.

I did feel fearful during those times I gave in to the worry that I wouldn't achieve my dreams and that I would be deeply disappointed. God knows I have had a lot of disappointments in my life that I still have to work through to get back to joy. I also doubted myself. How high a bar of success should I aspire to . . . again? I wrestled with work-life balance because I was concerned about losing my freedom from having to work so hard. Such questions kept cropping up.

Even now, having started over again, I still ask myself, "What do I want?" I think it's a question that helps establish perspective and, by answering it, it reminds me WHY I wanted what I eventually came up with. I have learned to wonder and explore like my little granddaughter, Calielle, as she has the freedom to touch and discover life with simple curiosity and abandonment.

I will share here a few game-changer ideas, which benefited me greatly, to help you renew, refresh, and reset for the new future that awaits you.

- **Draw on Your Faith:** When you are struggling, and life has served you one knock too many, draw on your faith, your religion, and belief system that anchors your life. Find the good in your life and be grateful for it. You may not feel as strong as you would like to be or believe you have to be to achieve success. Accept that it's par for the course to undergo moments when you feel weak, doubtful, or afraid. I made a sign in my office that read, *"Don't Believe Everything You Think."* It was a good reminder that my fears and doubts just weren't true, and that I didn't have to believe these thoughts or take them to heart. My faith in God is my daily focus because I believe He loves me and has great plans for my life. A great Bible verse for this promise is, *For I know the plans I have for you, declares the Lord, plans to prosper you and not harm you, plans to give you hope and a future* (Jeremiah 29:11).

- **Live Courageously:** Life is not about standing still. When you connect with your purpose and destiny, you'll find courage. I say courage is like faith: It doesn't feel; it just acts. Courage can be misperceived as the absence of fear. That is not true. Courage is taking action in spite of doubt and fear. What helps me when I need courage is to reflect on what the scriptures say: *" . . . with God, all things are possible"*; and *" . . . whatever is true, whatever is noble, whatever is right, whatever is just, whatever is pure, whatever is lovely, whatever is admirable—if anything is excellent or praiseworthy—think about such things."* This kind of faith and truth helps me to avoid doubt and to stay focused on what keeps me in a good positive frame of mind for success.

- **Get Comfortable with Feeling Uncomfortable:** If you're not uncomfortable, you are not growing. A certain degree of discomfort means you are either winning or learning, both of which are good states to be in. We often want to run from any kind of suffering—I know I do. But it's not realistic to think that every step you are taking is going to be fun and not challenging. Your expectations for this new beginning can help or hinder you. Expect this season in your life to be difficult; but the good that comes out of it is that you will grow and get through it, while becoming a much better and stronger person.

- **Release the Past:** Process any disappointment that you may still be feeling, that may be held over from the past. Let go of any bitterness from not having done better, or avoiding the divorce or the loss of a business. Don't waste energy crying about what has gone by; in fact, stop dwelling in the past. Make a deliberate choice to be better from here on, and not bitter and angry. One of my mottos is, "*Be better, not bitter.*"

- **Change Your Focus to the Present and Future:** There is a brand-new future awaiting you, awaiting your discovery. If you find yourself waking up with vague, undefined anxiety about possible problems that may or may not happen, change your focus. Be intentional, be deliberate, and focus on what will strengthen you, not what debilitates you. T. Harv Eker often says, "*Where attention goes, energy flows and results show.*" Shift your focus so that your life will head toward what you desire. In that same theme, I wrote on one of my vision boards: "*What I focus on will expand.*"

- **Believe in Yourself:** Confidence is your friend in starting over. In fact, make it your new best friend. Keep it close to your heart. Trust your own vision, listen to the voice of your intuition, pray for higher guidance, celebrate your strengths, and know deep down that there is no one else in this world that is exactly like you, and your contribution to the world is unique to you. You've more talent, skills, and gifts within you than you know. So, go for it. The sky is NOT the limit.

- **Rest and Recover:** Set aside some time to recharge in any way you can. Your physical body needs a break—the decision to start over can in itself be highly stressful, but once you've decided to do so, take a break to revive your mental and emotional batteries, and let yourself breathe. Go away on a personal retreat, realize the long-desired vacation, or if your budget is an issue, go for a long walk in the woods or rent a bike to explore nature trails. Don't feel that you have to overcommit and fill your days immediately with appointments or meeting up with people you need advice from. Leave yourself space and time to decompress, and out of the quiet and stillness, new and imaginative ideas, which may not have occurred to you before, will have the space to surface.

- **Get Back on Track if You Slip:** You are not perfect, so if you do find yourself slipping back into old habits, such as procrastination, recognize that you have strayed a little from your new path, and get back on track. It's as simple as that. Starting over is not seamless; there'll be bumps and hiccups, but there's no need to beat yourself up—just dust yourself off and resume your journey.

- **Choose the Right Language:** Create the right mindset with the words you say and think. Some people say that times like these are for you to "discover" yourself, but I believe in saying that this is a time to "create." You can create a new you when starting over. The old you belongs to the past and should stay there, regardless of why you are starting over, by choice or by lack of choice. Ask yourself these questions at this time of a redo: Who do you want to be? What do you want to be like? What do you want to accomplish, and be known for and sought out for? Ask yourself these questions, because the answers will create impactful outcomes that will ripple throughout all of the rest of your life. Who you are becoming determines what you'll reap later.

- **Start Over for All the Right Reasons:** This is your time to do what you want and need, not because someone else needs you to. You might have to walk a path you've never considered before, or one that's less traveled; but if it calls to you, follow your heart, follow your intuition, and trust your faith.

- **Recognize That You Are Not Alone:** There are countless stories of women who had to start over, now and throughout history. They lost their jobs or businesses, went bankrupt, got divorced, lost their health, had to move, and many other reasons. You are not unusual, nor alone. You can do this. You can start over.

- **Find Inspiration from Role Models:** One of the easiest ways to get inspired is to read about women who have succeeded in starting over. There are some good books that are biographies and autobiographies of women who decided to design their futures, and became immensely successful doing it. They had their own share of challenges, and reading about how such women overcame their blocks to achieve financial success, will give you hope and confidence to stride forward. There are a number of books that I have enjoyed and recommend: the biography about the revolutionary clothing designer, Chanel, called *Chanel and Her World*, by her friend, Edmonde Charles-Roux; and the historical biography, *On Her Own Ground*, about Madam C. J. Walker, written by A'Leiia Bundles, Walker's great-great-granddaughter. The daughter of enslaved parents, African-American Walker was a mover and shaker, and became a highly successful entrepreneur, philanthropist, and social activist. She has the honor of being listed in the Guinness World Records as the first female self-made millionaire. Another is *Miracles Happen*, an autobiography by Mary Kay Ash. She's one of America's most dynamic businesswomen. Through her uncomplicated formula for success—God first, family second, and career third—she built her dream company that achieved more than one billion in sales, and an international sales force of over 800,000. These women found the courage to buck the trend to create businesses that the world had never seen before, and have been all the better for it since.

Make small changes, day in and day out; take tiny steps every day, until you know you're on the right path. The key is to take action; there's nothing too small that you do that doesn't move you forward. Staying still and remaining stagnant is of no help.

Fun Exercise

1. Take an inventory of who you are, and create a success list of your experiences, expertise, skills, gifts, talents, leadership positions, volunteer history, awards, recognitions, and successes. Include compliments you've received, what people have indicated they like about you, obstacles you have overcome, and victories achieved, small and large. This list is meant to reinforce in you the belief that you're not starting over empty-handed. You are more equipped than you think, and you are stronger and more resilient than you believe. Look at this list often, when you need an extra boost of motivation.

2. Stretch your boundaries. Go out and do something you've never done before, and share your experience with a friend. Always wanted to paint? Join an online course? Afraid of speaking in public? Video yourself baking, cooking, singing, dancing, playing the piano, or talking about your garden, and share it on video or social media platforms of your choice. Breaking out of your comfort zone is necessary to help you leap into something new.

Women Starting Over and Moving Up

Success Story from Jeremee Quijada to Nora Ellen

> I'm so grateful for coaching with Nora, because she always says that her ceiling is my springboard. I did not know that I had an entrepreneur spirit inside of me or that I could be a successful businesswoman, until Nora enlightened me to what natural gifts and talents I have, from the success I was already producing. I feel her support as I venture into this new territory for myself, with my new business igniting my mindset to higher income potential. When I first started coaching with Nora, I didn't even know that I had entrepreneurship exploding inside of me. I was just trying to earn money, with very little vision of what I was doing. She was able to light a fire that I didn't even know existed, and now it's burning at an exponential rate, along with my income. I feel like she lights the fire under my wings, where I'm soaring into uncharted territories in my personal life and in business. Her coaching has caused me to always look up, onward and forward, instead of fearing the future or looking at the past. She encourages me to run ahead. She has really stirred my business passion, and there have been times that if I didn't have her as a cheerleader to push forward, I maybe would have gotten sidetracked by discouragement and the hard actions, where ultimately growth and success is born.

Chapter 3

Preparing for Your New Journey

"If you fail to plan, you are planning to fail."
—Benjamin Franklin

The decision is made. You have decided to step away from the past and forge ahead into a new future.

But when you really get down to it, what do you do next? The future is brimming over with possibilities, but which are the ones you need to pursue? How do you consciously identify new and creative ways to successfully generate income? How do you make informed financial choices at a time of great uncertainty?

You certainly don't want to run yourself ragged by chasing opportunities that turn into dead ends; neither do you want to overlook possibilities that empower you to create wealth and prosperity. Some of you may be like me: I just want to jump in and go!

> **Here's a tip:** Be willing to take some time out to write some goals and plan out your road map. Some of you may balk at this. Why, you may ask; why not play it by ear?

Why prepare before starting your do-over or planning your moving up?

Preparing Is Taking the Right Action

When you go on a vacation—let's say to Hawaii—you wouldn't be packing snow boots or heavy parkas, would you? You would have flip-flops, beachy dresses, and Hawaiian shirts and shorts in your luggage. If you were going skiing, you would be loading your car with downhill or cross-country snow skis, snowboards, snow goggles, and ski poles. You wouldn't be packing tents, camping cookware, a mini-stove, or a hammock. Your destination dictates what you need in order to have the most fun, and what is the most fitting for where you are heading.

The same applies to where you are headed now. You don't want to take useless, inappropriate baggage along with you. If anything, you want to disown the old junk—emotional, mental, and habitual—that got you going down the old road that led to nowhere.

Remember, without proper preparation, you'll quickly run out of motivation. So, now that we are on the same page, what are some of the old pieces of junk that you need to disown? What kind of mental and emotional reset do you need?

Make it About the Journey and Not the End

The very first thing you owe to yourself is to *commit*! If just reading the word "commit" is scary for some of you, you'll need to redefine for yourself what commitment means. To some of you, committing means being tied down or bogged down by a burden of responsibilities. You are giving up your freedom in exchange for what? A small possibility of success with great risk? What if the new venture fails? Why put yourself through the pain of disappointment, struggle, and sorrow again?

I previously thought I had committed to change, but it didn't work because I didn't understand what I was committing to, or the real purpose behind making a commitment. I was hoping for something simple or easy, something magical, without any real work or understanding—like getting fast food. It's not enough to just say you will commit, or to tell someone you're committing, without first deeply reflecting on what you are willing to commit to and become.

Commitment can feel confining and limiting. Yet without commitment, you may encounter too much chaos, and your way forward may be haphazard rather than carefully thought out, leading to poor outcomes or even disappointments and failure. Some of you may, on the other hand, be afraid of success. You may be agonizing over losing friends who may be envious of your success, or having to work so hard that you turn into a workaholic, sacrificing work-life balance to get your new venture off the ground.

As you can see, you can easily come up with reasons to derail your do-over. But if you have a firm commitment, the ironclad resolve will help you keep going even when the road is bumpy and you feel like giving up.

Here's an easy little exercise that helped me greatly: Write down your commitment, and share it with someone close to you. Explain that this is your statement of commitment to starting over and to reaching success. I did this with a close friend, and I had a good laugh as I read it to her, but I was determined to grow. It was both fun and scary at the same time because, by speaking it out loud, someone else would know about it and would hold me accountable.

Just writing it down and speaking it out loud will help empower you to move forward. As a daily reminder, pin or tape your commitment statement on a wall or white board to remind yourself of the promise you have made to yourself.

Commitment may initially feel stifling and burdensome, but if you stick it out, it can actually turn into freedom. Understand that sometimes what you avoid doing is precisely what you need to do. An action that is outside your level of comfort, may be exactly the thing you need to do to achieve a different level of success. It's like a seed that has to die before it can come to life. A bud can die on the vine or it may bloom magnificently. After blossoming, the flower drops to the ground and gets buried in the soil. But the nutrients that are fed to the soil from the dead blossoms, are recycled into the plant, which then comes back to life when adequately fertilized and watered.

We often have to discipline ourselves to get something done, especially if it's having to carry out something that lies outside our normal comfort zones. That kind of action may not come naturally or easily to you, but it is important that you commit to carrying it out to create momentum in your forward progress.

Otherwise, by fearing to act outside of your lane, you will just be standing still at a time when you need the forward impetus. I am not suggesting you do something that lacks integrity. What I am referring to is doing something brand new. Or, something awkward, like politely serving someone who may not deserve it, or treating with love someone who may be hateful to you.

Letting Go

Only look back once at the past events that got you to where you are now. Give yourself a bit of time to grieve over your losses, but then you have to move on. What happened to you—any loss or failure that got you to this hard place—is not who you are. Those events happened in your life, but they are not who you are, so do not identify with them. Looking back and hanging on to unresolved issues holds you back. Instead, choose deliberately to have a fresh start. Hold your head up and look forward to the future with new eyes. It is good to acknowledge the lessons of history so that you don't repeat the mistakes, but don't sulk and indulge in a pity party. The only person you hurt when you overwhelm yourself with negativity and self-blame is you.

To let go, differentiate between healthy grieving and an unhealthy obsession that can only lead to bitterness. Be willing to try a different way of living. If you need to reflect on the past, give yourself the permission to do so for an hour or a day, but that's it. Place a time limit on indulging in the past. Be proactive about letting go, with constructive steps such as going to a counselor, journaling your feelings and emotions, or talking with a friend who is a good listener. Write your hurts down with a marker on a balloon, and then release it; or scribble them on a piece of paper, which you then burn. Do whatever is necessary to let go, in order to focus forward.

Burying the Hatchet, Which Really Means to Forgive

It's not the easiest thing to do, I'll admit. I have had many times in my life where I had to forgive others. It's way easier to want to lash out in anger, or want to extract justice for those who have harmed you. You may have valid reasons for wanting to inflict suffering on someone who has harmed you: to stop them from doing the same to someone else, or to compel them to change and stop their harmful behavior. Or you may want to get payback, so that you can feel better about being mistreated, abused, betrayed, robbed, violated, or laid off without cause.

It's common for well-meaning people to say "forgive and forget," but I say it's the worst thing you can offer or receive as advice. Your brain is like a virtual recorder, and horrible experiences are often accompanied by strong emotions, and tend to be deeply imprinted.

However, the act of forgiving is different. And, yes, it is an act, an action. Forgiveness is more about finding freedom for yourself, rather than for the wrongdoer. Forgiveness is recognizing that you were treated wrongly, but you are not going to let the wrongdoers control your life and steal your happiness. It does not mean you have to trust them again or try your hardest to repair a broken relationship. There are times when you have to walk away from something that defies fixing or reconciliation. It also doesn't mean you have to continue to take the abuse. *Forgiveness means you let them off the hook; you let go of needing something bad to happen to them to just even the score. Forgiveness is getting closure for yourself. It's for your own freedom in every way.*

I remember the first time I heard this definition of forgiveness. It made sense to me and was even a relief. I am not forgetting what happened, and this does not erase the wrongdoing. Instead, I am choosing to let them off my hook so that I don't have to be burdened with reprisals to make me feel better. Bitterness is the opposite of forgiveness. Bitterness and resentment can RUIN your life, your health, your looks, your relationships, your success, and your future. Unforgiveness makes you unhappy because it shackles you to the past. The happiest people I know are forgiving people.

Freedom is a choice we make, and it is up to you to choose. As I write these words, I have tears in my eyes, as I fully know how hard it can be to let go of the hurt and forgive. I have had to forgive both my first and second husband for the hurt they caused me, and for shipwrecking our marriage, even though we had vowed to be together "till death do us part." Forgiving them was a process; it wasn't just a one-time event. But when I have forgiven others for the wrongs they have done to me, it brings peace and inner freedom to ME. And because I know I am not perfect and have hurt others, I want them to forgive me too.

This does not mean you don't file charges against a molester, or take action for justice in court if you were robbed or raped. That is not what I am referring to here. Forgiveness is creating freedom for yourself—freedom in your heart so you are not held back by someone who has wronged you—so that you can move on. You can think more clearly and be emotionally more intelligent.

Sometimes there are layers of forgiveness, but forgiveness leads to the emotional and mental freedom that you need in order to succeed in your own life. You are not hurting the other person by holding on; you are only hurting yourself. Holding someone hostage in your heart and mind does not hurt them; it only hurts you. The people of your past may never change, and you may never ever get an apology from them. Instead, for your own life and future, learn to forgive. It is a process, but it begins with a deliberate decision to forgive.

I also have needed to forgive myself for mistakes I have made in my life. There are counselors and good books written entirely on forgiveness and the benefits of letting go. Someone who I respect for what she lived through is Joyce Meyer, now an acclaimed author and speaker. She was horribly and repeatedly raped and molested by her father, from when she was 3 years old until she left home at 18. This is unthinkable and unconscionable for her father to do this to his own daughter. Yet, she said, *"Harboring unforgiveness is a result of anger toward someone that has hurt you, and this can hinder your life."* Amongst her many bestselling books, one which has helped countless women is called *Do Yourself a Favor . . . Forgive: Learn How to Take Control of Your Life Through Forgiveness.*

Forgiveness isn't easy but it leads to great results. Forgiveness means freedom for your soul, especially when you understand that it's to make it about relieving you from the heavy pain and sorrow, not about the ones that had hurt you. It's about being able to move forward in your new start, with a lighter heart. It frees up your power, heals your hurting body, mind and spirit. And if you have read all the way to the end of this important section of this book, good for you. I commend and congratulate you for reading through this difficult part and being willing to help yourself to one of the most important ways for starting over. Holding grudges will never serve you in any way, including financially.

Right about now, you may be wanting to check out and slip into what I call "the zombie zone." This is the zone I get into when I don't want to think or feel or do what is required of me because something got triggered from my past. It's a good thing to be aware of when you are choosing to blank out what is uncomfortable—awareness of when you are in the zombie zone is your first step to snapping out of it and work through the healing you need.

It's natural to get stuck along the way of a new start, since you've never walked this road before. It can seem easier to just turn on the TV and veg out at times of indecision and stress. A little time out is okay, but don't make vegging out your default mode. That won't leave you feeling strengthened, nor will it empower you in any way. Be aware of how and what you are thinking of. Instead, put a time limit on vegging out and be willing to invest in yourself: read, learn new things, and engage with people who may be able to help.

Self-Care for a Healthy You

In going on this new journey, you will need energy. Take an inventory of habits that will help you. For example, are you eating healthily? Is there a type of nutrient-dense food you can add to your daily diet, and one you can eliminate to get to a healthier, stronger you? It's a good habit to avoid comfort foods, because most of them are stacked with sugars and carbs that don't add much to sustainable long-term energy. What I do when I want something sweet or want to indulge when I am not hungry, is to chew on a mint. There is something about minty flavoring that takes the edge off the urge to eat.

Take an inventory of your nutritional habits. Are you drinking 8 glasses of water a day to stay sufficiently hydrated? Are you getting out for a walk in the fresh air, or exercising regularly? Take an afternoon power nap if you need to. Have a time in your mind when you need to get ready to go to bed.

Develop a ritual that prepares you for bed and falling asleep quickly. Electronics and TV can interrupt your circadian cycle and falling asleep. Here is something better you can do each night before settling in to sleep. Write out a list of your successes, big and small, that you accomplished during the day. Think about all the things you did well, be it drinking an extra glass of water or getting a new interview.

We tend to think about our problems before we go to bed, which in turn deprives us of a good night's sleep and leaves us waking up in the past. It's hardly the right start when your first thought in the morning is about your problems. Don't let your subconscious programming sabotage the start of your day. Intentionally choose the thoughts that support you, not sabotage you. Take care of yourself; choose habits that help you balance and thrive—you're the best person for the job.

This is the right place to mention a free mood enhancer for greater success: *expressing gratitude*. Yes, being thankful. Have appreciation for what you have, what you know, for those you love, and for where you live. Happy people are grateful, content people, and they are successful. You can practice gratitude at any moment. It really is an inspired gift, one that God gave us to help us when the going gets tough. When we give thanks, happy hormones are released into our bodies. Gratitude is a choice, and it's easy and simple to do. Sometimes when I feel overwhelmed, I stop, close my eyes, and think, "God, thank you. Just thank you. Thank you." That's all that is required to make me feel better. Try this: Say, "Thank you God for . . . , and thank you for. . . ." You will immediately feel better.

Express gratitude for something you had never thought to be thankful for. For one, I am thankful to you for giving me the honor of you reading my book. Another thing that I am very grateful and thankful for, especially in the middle of the night, is indoor plumbing. I know, it is a convenience we take for granted, but imagine having to run outdoors to the outhouse in the cold evenings!! Gratitude strengthens your resolve and your persistence. It's free and easy to do at any time. It's a great way to give yourself grace when you go through the difficulties and uncertainties that are bound to arise when you start over.

I am feeling really good right now just writing about being grateful and thankful. I remember when a friend texted me, "I appreciate you," after I did something for them. That made me feel so good. You make people on the other end of your thankfulness and appreciation feel good too. He didn't text, "I appreciate *it*." He instead wrote, "I appreciate *you*." That really touched me and changed my life. Now I tell, email, and text people all the time that I appreciate them. I appreciate <u>YOU</u>.

You can start over from a place of joy and purpose, or from pain and suffering. In this book, I seek to help you start over from a place of joy and purpose, because these new attitudes will carry you through to success, not pain and suffering. Nothing is permanent; you can change and adjust as you go along. I remember when

I first heard, "TFA," which stands for "Try, Fail, Adjust." Yes, I can try something, and change it if it doesn't work.

Create Your Very Own Starting Over Plan

Some people call it goal setting. I don't know about you, but I find writing out goals very hard to do. It feels restrictive to me. What if I fail or over-commit myself? Yet many success experts tell us to write down goals because "success leaves clues." This is a suggestion to study and model the behavior and strategies of high-achieving women, those who you want to end up like, to follow the clues they left on their path to success.

I opted for a different, more subtle goal setting approach. I started by writing out small, achievable goals, rather than a big, broad list. For example, a first step may be writing out how much money you want to make for the rest of the year; or something that you need, such as walking a mile a day. Pick attainable goals, because it is so encouraging when you achieve a goal.

This can also be a good time to get your dreams going again. What do you want? Why do you want that? Don't worry about how to get there, the future will work when the why part is clear. I find that if I go to the heart of the why, then I can identify my goals more easily. I suggest starting with where you want to end up, and working backwards from there. What helps me with my goals is to "time block," where I commit to using a certain hour for a dollar-productive activity, such as generating leads or prospecting.

Write down your plan, and break it down with what works for you. I had bought an in-depth planner on the advice of a coach. This was a big stretch for me because I have struggled with how to carry over some big responsibilities, from day to day, or week to week. I decided to get a large dry erase board, and wrote the bigger tasks on it. I hung the board in my office and felt immediate relief to see my goals in a place where I could easily refer to them, rather than having them run around disorganized in my mind.

The white board helped to reframe my perspective on what I wanted and how to use my time wisely to get there. By having them up front and center, I could prioritize my goals and easily tweak and adjust them along the way. I love collaborating with other people, and by having my white board of goals in my office, it felt to me like I was collaborating with myself, which turned out to be a lot of fun.

Write down your goals and then break them into annual, monthly, weekly, and daily tasks. This would also be a good time to map out how you are going to save, give, and spend your money. Be intentional. And yes, I am talking about having a budget included with your goals.

I have never been fond of the word "budget," but I have learned that this kind of financial discipline yields many benefits. I don't want to get deep into budgeting here, as there are many sources you can tap into. Just find a system that works for you to get a smooth start. Keep your goals in a place where you can look at them daily, so that they sink deep into your subconscious mind and go to work for you.

One more thing before going on to Chapter 4: Choose a couple of friends to be your support circle during this time. These friends should commit to checking up on you and encouraging you when your commitment lags, and one of them should be the person to whom you read out your commitment. This is the right time to ask for help. Don't be shy about reaching out; generally, people are happy to help. You deserve to receive help because you have helped many others yourself.

Fun Exercise

With daily gratitude and appreciation, you will start over with the understanding that this is not an end but a new beginning.

Every morning while you lie in bed, before you open your eyes, express thanksgiving, making it a new habit.

For example, in my morning gratitude time, I thank God for my kids, grandchildren, my little fluffy dog, indoor plumbing, my sanctuary, and for a new day by which I get to make an impact on the lives of other women. And I do thank Him for something I have never thanked Him for prior, to help keep my mind renewed. When you do this, you will become more and more grateful and happier.

I do it with good news and bad news, thanking God that things will get better. Gratitude is so strengthening. It uplifts you physiologically, spiritually, and emotionally.

And just as crucially, gratitude wipes the slate clean because it places you in a position where you can say, truthfully to yourself, that you learned from the hard knocks. You can put the pain behind you and move forward to creating a positive vision for your life.

It is so rewarding to be on this journey with you. It's never too late to start over, because it's never too late to find and to do the things you need to make you happy. This time, you are making yourself the priority.

Chapter 4

You Have the Power to Take Control of Your Life

"As a woman thinks in her heart, so is she."
—Proverb modified by Nora Ellen,
to the feminine

A fresh start needs a clean slate. And the clean slate requires that you reset your mindset, from failure to success.

The classic self-help essay, *As a Man Thinketh,* by James Allen, postulates that the key to mastering your life comes from harnessing the power of your thinking. It's from this kind of power thinking that you cultivate an attitude of a successful person. Allen's piece, which is rooted in wisdom discussed in Chapter 23 of the Book of Proverbs, was written in 1903; and among some of his more profound statements is this quote: *"All that a man achieves and all that he fails to achieve is the direct result of his own thoughts."*

Without mastering your thoughts, you are held hostage to the cycle of disappointment and heartache that led you to wanting to start over. A fresh start is exactly what it means: You have to have a fresh mindset, a fresh set of emotions.

You have to change your mind, and you have to train your mind into believing in your capabilities and success. That is the game changer because, when you change your thoughts, you let go of the self-limiting beliefs, behaviors, and attitudes that you held in the past.

This all sounds very well and good, but you may be asking questions at this point: What do you have to do? How do you reset your mindset? How do you step into the bigger life that is awaiting you?

The Power of Thought

Let's first look at how fast thoughts whiz through your mind. What is the speed of thought? Science has made some guesses, but it is estimated that your brain takes less than a quarter of a millisecond to process external information. As a form of measure, a sprinter takes 150 milliseconds to react to the sound of the starting gun. In the time it takes you to take one breath, you would have gone through countless thoughts.

The key, therefore, to upgrading your mindset, is to control what and how you think.

Here are a few steps on how to manage that:

1. **Become conscious and aware**—Observe your thoughts and actions. This way, you live and act more from choice rather than from some old subconscious programming running through your mind that has been shaped by

your past experiences. Check your thoughts often. This is very crucial. Your thoughts are so powerful because they create the emotions that then determine how you behave and act throughout the day. Make deliberate choices to pick the thoughts that serve you and support your growth and your new path forward. I call this *power thinking*, which is way beyond positive thinking, because it is thinking that deepens your commitment to self-awareness and actual change.

2. **Ask the right questions**—This next step empowers you to own this new vision you are calling into your life. The questions you ask yourself will impact where you are heading, why are you heading there, and how you are getting there.

    - What am I thinking now?
    - Why am I thinking this, and where did it come from?
    - Is this from my past, and did I attach a meaning to it that is not serving me?
    - Why am I holding onto past mistakes?
    - Is this thought aligned with my vision? Is it a story that is helping me to move forward to greater fulfillment and achievement?

Understand that this is a lifelong process. When you are starting over, you may not see the desired changes immediately. I sometimes feel like the process of change is like turning around a gigantic container ship or huge aircraft carrier. To the observer, nothing seems to be perceptibly happening, even though the cogs and wheels are already in motion, but with time, the big ship turns around and heads toward a new destination.

You will too, as long as you understand that even when you are taking baby steps, you are still moving. This is not to belittle yourself or criticize, but to better understand where you are at and where you want to end up. Be kind to yourself and acknowledge that to every season, there is a reason.

Your Power Is Within, Not Outside Yourself

Too often, we believe what happens to us comes from the circumstances outside our control. And we cannot change the outcomes. It's true that changing a bad situation isn't possible, at least maybe not immediately possible for your liking. But you know what you can change, and it's something you can do immediately.

You can choose how you process and react to the situation, and what meaning you attach to it. You can wake up saying, "It's going to be a bad day because the weather is crummy," OR you can start your day by saying, "Even though it's chilly out, I choose to enjoy this day." Of course, you'll be impacted by an external event—you are human—but the power rests within you to not dwell on self-defeating thoughts.

Don't look for an outside outcome to be fixed to mitigate your disappointment at any given moment; you fix yourself by changing your mindset instead. The longer you allow such thoughts of regret or discontent to dwell in your mind, the faster they rob you of peace, joy, and life's satisfaction.

When you become aware of the power to choose, that's when you make the powerful changes to become the best version of yourself.

Unbottle the Emotions

Women are thought to be more emotional than men, but that's more because we feel emotions more clearly. But are we allowing our emotions to control us?

Recognize that there is absolutely no shame in expressing your emotions, but it's only when you let your emotions dictate your decisions and actions that they become a problem. Give yourself permission to unbottle your emotions as a means of controlling them. Do so in any number of ways: by writing them down, journaling, or sharing with a friend.

I write down all my emotions, and I let go of what I feel. I will ask myself:

- How am I feeling?
- Am I feeling hurt or disappointed?
- Am I feeling confused or disrespected?
- Do I feel as if I am failing myself?
- What am I afraid of?

I find putting my emotions down on paper very useful, because it's a visual guide that helps me pinpoint what emotions are running wayward through me, and allows me to identify where they are coming from. When we can pinpoint those emotions, we can trace them back to a point of origin. I avoid letting myself get stuck in replaying the emotions over and over again. I am not controlled by my emotions; I am intentional to use my will on how to live my life.

It happens to all of us: Something triggers a memory of a disappointment, and it plays over and over in your mind. And the bitter taste of a relived regret will affect your next decisions and actions unless you process it and let go of it.

Of course, I have had disappointments, but I continue to purposely focus my mind to look for new and wonderful opportunities. There are always loads of opportunities out there. Install self-powering thoughts; use your power thinking and you'll be able to spot the doors opening. Can you imagine being able to spot a potential opening, if your mind is drowning in negative emotions of frustration, discontent, and distress?

This is necessary inner work. Many people think that what's necessary is to put in the outer work—boots on the ground, knocking on doors, sending out resumes, networking furiously—without putting in the inner work. I say that you first need to put in the time for your inner work, because you are the root of your financial success or failure. When the ground is properly cultivated, through minding your thoughts, processing your emotions, and choosing an empowering mindset, that's when you reap the fruits of success.

Dump Those Self-Limiting Beliefs

They are insidious, those self-limiting beliefs. They bubble along; they take hold in your consciousness, and you hear them as voices in your head, but you don't necessarily recognize them as being toxic. But they are. Self-limiting beliefs are conjured out of your own mind, and they hold you back. You hear the voices say, "You're not good enough; you blew your only chance; no one wants to hire you; you lack the experience," and so on, over and over again.

There are times when I think I am drifting aimlessly, or I am procrastinating because I have nothing to offer. When such beliefs bubble up, I take a pause. I stop what I am doing, and I pay heed to the voices in my head and begin an exploration.

Okay, what is this? What's bringing about these depressed feelings? Why are they recurring? One of my explorations actually yielded a surprising result. I found that I was afraid of success because I might lose friends who are struggling financially when I succeed in making more money than they are.

Of course, friends matter, but do you want them to become baggage on your journey to a bigger and more expanded life? Friends who don't cheer you on because you are doing better than they are, and who become envious of your starting over, are not friends who will support or empower you. You may feel loyalty toward them, but there will come a time when you have to choose—you cannot be afraid of losing friends, or you are going to stay stuck or lose out on the tremendous possibilities that are waiting for you.

You may be afraid of success because you are afraid of failing; so you avoid the risk, you play it safe, and you don't take the plunge. You stay in a rut, which is thinly disguised as your comfort zone. But when you are starting over, you need to put on your big girl pants and step outside of the safety of your comfort zone.

I would like to leave you with this thought: *Every moment you spend doubting or criticizing yourself is a moment that you've forever lost, a moment you could have used instead actively making responsible, life enhancing choices.*

Rethink Comfort

You may think your comfort zone is a safe place to be in, but it's actually a place where mediocrity and fear live. As humans, we thrive when we are challenged. Yes, some comfort and routines are necessary, but if they become the end-all-and-be-all, you are choking your own growth.

Your success—your money thermostat—is inversely linked to the size of your comfort zone. The bigger the zone, the less financial success you'll have. Let's look at a few ways in which your unwillingness to step out of your comfort zone traps you.

An example might be that you want a promotion, but you are afraid of speaking up and asking your boss for more responsibilities. You want to make new friends, but you are too shy to step up to a stranger. You want to lose weight, but you are too embarrassed to step into a yoga class. Do you see what I am getting at?

You have to be willing to embrace a certain degree of discomfort, and do what is uneasy and maybe even unnerving, to become unstuck. When you stay glued to your comfort zone, you are letting your self-limiting beliefs take control of your life. Do what you must do in order to let go of the things that hold you back, most of which are in your mind.

I call the pesky doubts that run around in our heads, "ANTS"— my acronym for "automatic negative thoughts." In many ways, the ANTS are like the little insects that are busy running here and running there, without our fully being aware of them. But that's where the comparison ends. At most, you may get a bite or two out of the ants, and while the bite may itch for a while, the irritation goes away. But not ANTS—if you don't stop them, they take over your life.

In Chapter 3, I described a simple ritual in which you write down your fears on a balloon, with a big marker pen. And you release the balloon and let the winds carry it away.

Your mind is your biggest asset, but it can also be your biggest hindrance. Unless you consciously retrain your mindset, your mind is primed to protect you by having you stick to what is routine and safe.

Here's a tip: Take one small risk every day. Travel a different way to work, or wear a bright color if you normally prefer dark clothes. If you're a shy person, step up and strike a conversation with a stranger. It could be as simple as saying, "What a beautiful dog you have," and seeing where it goes. The conversation may just end there, but by taking small ventures outside of your comfort zone, you begin to stretch yourself and wake up your courage, and you'll gain in confidence to take even bigger steps next time.

Simplify Your Health With Choices

They are called comfort foods for a reason—they make us feel better for those few minutes—but are they really helping? The sugar rush from the chocolate bar might help pick you up from the dumps, but then you'll be dealing with the sugar slump afterwards.

Be aware if you are self-medicating with food, or using other coping mechanisms like alcohol or substance abuse. I like my chocolate, potato chips, and Pepsi, and there are times when I allow myself those small indulgences, but not when they are meant to tamp down a fear or dull emotional distress.

Comfort eating may reduce stress temporarily because you are replacing distress with a food high, but when used as a crutch, over the long run, it does little to improve your self-esteem, and it puts yet another problem on your plate: weight gain or even diabetes from unhealthy eating habits.

Check and see if you are self-medicating with things like too much mindless TV, movies or even pornography. Many people delude themselves when they think that they are "vegging" out by watching, and putting the distressing negative thoughts on hold. But the truth is that your brain is still working behind the scenes, and you are really not getting the rest and reviving you need.

Music soothes the wildest beast, and it's one of the healthiest forms of mental escape. But even then, you have to make choices that support you. For example, a lot of the top music hits are all about romance, unwanted or unrequited love, love and loss, and so on. As a single woman, these are hardly the themes I want to listen to. I gain nothing from listening to such lyrics; if anything, they seem to cloud up my mind.

Instead, I would rather listen to music that uplifts me, enhances my creativity, and strengthens my focus. It's been proven that the old Gregorian songs and chants alleviate fatigue and depression. Baroque music, such as the works of Vivaldi, Bach, and Handel, and classics from Mozart are thought to strengthen focus and concentration. There is also the book of Psalms set to music. I enjoy some of the old hymns and Christian music that comforts and brings me peace.

Your Thought Treasure Chest

Here is a powerful tool that you can immediately work on or access. Build for yourself, in your own mind, a thought treasure chest, a place where you store positive, funny, wise, and life-affirming thoughts that you can draw on when you need to replace negative thoughts.

In comic strips, the artist always draws a thought bubble over the heads of the characters to illustrate what they are thinking about. Imagine that when you have a negative thought, there is a thought bubble over your head, and you rub off the unhappy thought with an eraser. Next, you open your thought treasure chest and pluck out a fitting positive thought, and you insert it into your thought bubble. It sounds a little silly but it works.

Your treasure chest should be filled with wonderful memories of successes, awards, recognition, accomplishments, or times when you laughed so much your sides ached. Insert, into the chest, powerful affirmations that change your brain chemistry, such as, "I am successful," "I am loved," "I am courageous," "I can do this."

Add other affirmations that strengthen your determination in starting over, such as, "This is the perfect time to start over," "Opportunities abound everywhere," "I'm open to and I recognize opportunities when they are presented to me." Fill your thought treasure chest to the top with many beautiful thoughts that glimmer and glow like real jewels, gold and silver.

When you need a boost, shop in your treasure chest to retrieve a powerful affirmation. Your mind is like a muscle. The more you train it to turn to positive affirmations, the more readily it will retrieve positive thoughts at a moment's notice when you need them most.

For example, we are living through the throes of a world pandemic, which has led to closures of businesses, stalled global economies, and people being furloughed from their jobs. Yet there are people who are making money during such hard times. These are the ventilator makers, online meeting companies, the businesses that make personal protection equipment, and even restaurants that restyled themselves to offer pick-up and delivery services. Some online companies, for example, have had their sales soar or been chalking up a string of new highs in their stock prices, and produced record profits because they benefitted from the shift in consumer spending, from brick and mortar stores to online purchasing.

Even at the worst of the Great Depression, in the early 20th century, people continued to buy lipstick and used their last few nickels to get a bottle of coke.

It's only when you view the world through a positive lens that you can see opportunities and doors opening, even while everyone around you is saying that the sky has fallen. This is where your thought treasure chest comes in.

I shall write more about these kinds of affirmations in Chapter 5, but you can start filling your thought treasure chest at any time. Why not now?

Fear Forward

Fight, flight or freeze, however you respond when afraid, isn't unusual. Fear is an emotion triggered by a perceived threat. Fear is not to be ignored or squashed. It's a normal emotion and you can use it to your advantage or drown in a phobia. What's nice is you do have a choice how to respond, instead of react. It is the same with anxiety and worry. The important thing is that you know yourself when it comes to what you fear and worry about, what triggers you and why. In knowing this, you are better able to understand and help yourself with the right thinking where you are not dominated and lead by fear and worry.

When you excavate your self-limiting beliefs, you have no choice but to come face to face with your fears. That happened to me recently. Inexplicably, I became anxious about my financial situation. Why was this coming up? I took a pause and asked myself why I was feeling this. What was really bothering me, and what was at the root of this anxiety?

I dug deep and came to the realization that I was nursing a fear that I would be a financial burden to my wonderful children and their spouses, who would have to take care of me in my old age or if I was somehow incapacitated. That fear played at the back of my mind, but once I isolated it, I could do something about it.

Fears come in all forms and shapes. For you, it could be a fear of abandonment or fear of rejection. For your best friend, it could be a fear of poverty or a fear of failure. If these fears are allowed to fester, they take root and they strangle you. It's undeniably uncomfortable to address your fears, but it's worth it because, by confronting them directly, you rob them of their stranglehold on you.

In an earlier chapter, I pointed out that our fears rarely ever come true. Fears are a distortion of faith, and they loom as big as your mind allows them to be. Remember, what you truly desire is on the other side of fear.

Dump the Imposter Syndrome

Another thing that I want you to do is to dump what I call the fraud syndrome. It's also known as the imposter syndrome, in which a successful person like you doubts her achievements, and attributes it to luck and timing, and not to talent and ability. When the imposter syndrome strikes, you worry incessantly that what you've achieved is not repeatable, and that you're soon to be found out for the incompetent, incapable underachiever that you truly are.

Of course, you have made mistakes; you are only human, and you have flaws like we all do. But you also possess a unique set of God-given talents that no one else has. When you allow the fraud syndrome to get hold of you, you are denying yourself the opportunities that can only be unlocked by your distinctive set of skills.

If this fraud syndrome has struck you, stop and realize that once again, it's fear speaking. It's fear disguised as a fraud syndrome, and it's just a story that you tell yourself. And if you don't know how to disown it, I recommend digging into your thought treasure chest for affirmations to flip the switch.

Manage Your Expectations

Are you asking too much of yourself? Women tend to do this because they feel they have to overperform and overdo in a world in which inequities still exist in terms of salary, promotion opportunities, and even public expectation. I am guilty of that, and I often set myself up for disappointment because, for whatever reason, I never got around to finishing my to-do list—maybe I was derailed or sidetracked, or I had to put out an unexpected fire.

Manage the burden of expectations that you place on yourself, so that it isn't so heavy that you can't take a step forward without buckling down, and not so light that it requires no effort or new learning from you. You have to constantly tweak your expectations. I've said it before: We, as humans, thrive in the face of challenge, because we sense that challenges make us grow and force us to tap into our limitless potential.

As you adjust your expectations, remember these tips:

- Don't try to live up to someone else's expectations. It's your life; your needs and motivations are what are important.
- Set your bar at a high enough level that you're willing to say yes to the new inherent challenges.
- Uplevel your expectations once you've cleared a hurdle or met a challenge.
- Mind your expectations of others—what are you expecting by way of help from your friends and family during this time of starting over?

- Be willing to communicate clearly and explain what you need from others, but don't be so reliant that you are unable to move forward if help doesn't come, or at least not in the shape you expect of it.

Focus Your Mind

I keep dry erase boards around my house. They are both decorative and functional, and I write uplifting quotes on them as a way of focusing my mind on what truly matters to me. And I can erase the messages and write new ones on each board.

Right now, the quote on the board in my office is, *"Where I focus is where my day will go."* This message speaks to me because it reminds me that we have to be intentional about what we turn our thoughts and focus to, because what we focus on will expand, and it will grow.

As you are reading this book, are you focusing your mental energies on power thinking, or are you wasting away your mind and time in trivialities, doubts, and fears? If focusing your mind doesn't come naturally to you, remember that it takes practice. You need to lift weights to build muscles in your body, and you need to exercise to build your mind's focus muscles.

Having an uplifting quote or message as a point of focus helps me greatly. I lean more toward being a free spirit, and I've conducted business by the seat of my pants. I am prone to jumping from one thought to another, and when I find I am getting increasingly distracted, I pull myself back to redirect the flow of my thoughts. For example, when I am distracted by something upsetting, or overwhelmed by negativity, I stop and think or say out loud, "Yes, yes, yes, let's do this," or "Happy thoughts, happy thoughts, happy thoughts, let's go!" until it short circuits the negativity. Also, a quick "thank you, thank you" thought gratitude break helps me to refocus. These actions will activate the frontal lobe of your brain, which will get your focus back.

It's an easy way to flip the switch. Do whatever works best for you. I know someone who will count numbers backwards. By counting down from 5 to 1, she says she redirects her mental focus away from negativity. I think it is a good start, but it stops short of directing one to happier thoughts to get back into action. If you tend to dwell on what hasn't worked, or are bogged down by unproductive self-criticism, change the direction of your mental energy by saying or thinking a simple phrase until you've altered the flow of your thoughts.

Reward Yourself

You will come across hurdles and bumps on the road when you start over. Some of them will be easily overcome, some may just be tedious tasks, and some may require that you step far away from your comfort zone. When the going seems tough, you may find yourself slacking.

Since being in real estate, I have had to rake through hundreds of names in a client database, and make a similar number of cold calls. It was an onerous task, which frankly was tedious for a free-spirited person like me. My solution was to create rewards for myself to boost my motivation. I did so by visualizing what I would buy for myself when the hundred calls finally led to income-generating transactions. And after completing the goal of all the calls, I bought myself something as a reward.

You don't have to choose expensive rewards either, but as women, we tend to neglect our own needs, to care for someone else. So I say to go ahead; reward yourself with something lavish! Having a reward helps you get over those days when you feel weighed down or when it feels as if it's too much, because having something pleasant waiting for you at the end, makes the journey worthwhile.

Live Loved, Love Yourself

When the going gets really tough, I find strength by drawing on the love that I receive from God and the people close to me, and by thinking of the people I love. In my life, I make it a priority to "live loved," by reminding myself that I am surrounded and supported by wonderful people and I get to support them, too.

There was a time in my own journey of starting over that I felt I had reached the end of my rope. I stood in my kitchen crying, worn out and totally exhausted. I felt I had nothing left in the tank. As I stood on the edge of this precipice, I thought of my kids and how much they loved me and how much I loved them. My thoughts then flew to how blessed I was that I had support from the most wonderful people: my neighbors, my church community, and the different groups with which I am associated, such as my book club. The more I felt loved, the more I felt strength returning to me. It was a simple but profoundly powerful shift.

Millions of people around the world feel alone and depressed because they lack connection. They crave it, but they do not know how to find it, and they look to fleeting experiences and substances to drown out the overwhelming sense of sadness.

You are loved and appreciated by more people than you think. You are loved by God, your Creator; and you, the reader of my book, are loved by me. Hopefully, you love yourself too, because self-love is a very powerful force. It's the source of your courage, your motivation, and your sense of purpose. When you have self-love, you require less to be given to you from the outside, and you are very grateful when you do receive love from another.

Can you imagine what the world would look like if we all loved God, each other, and ourselves? There would be no need to expect to be taken care of by another, or to lash out in anger from feeling unloved. This actually comes from the two greatest commandments in the Bible. It sounds simple, but it's the truth. I want you to live feeling loved.

There is a difference between feeling lonesome and feeling lonely. These are merely emotions, not conditions. These emotions are coming from the way you think about yourself. Feeling lonely suggests that no one loves you, and that you are abandoned and you're not worth caring for. Lonesome means that you are on your own. I live by myself and, sometimes, I feel lonesome; and during those times, I would welcome the presence of another person to talk to and to do things with. If you struggle with loneliness, think and say this out loud every time you feel lonely:

- I am special
- I am wanted
- I am God's treasure
- I am important
- I am loved
- I have destiny

- I have great purpose
- I am needed
- I matter

Then be intentional about developing more loving relationships in your life.

There are so many ways to live loved. Think of all the people who love you—not just your immediate family, but also extended members, including grandparents who may have moved on, or uncles, aunts, and cousins. Don't forget them.

Next, there are so many ways to make friends in this day and age. Approach someone at a networking event, and strike up a conversation by saying, "Hey, you look like somebody who would be interesting to talk to." Invite them out for a coffee or tea. Join gardening clubs, develop a hobby, and join a group of hobbyists.

Recently, when I found my social networks and communities changing, I decided to start a women's entrepreneur mastermind on a smaller scale, a group that I wanted to be a part of but couldn't find meetings in person. It was easy to put this kind of group together, as many other women were feeling the same as I did, with the desire to connect, grow, and learn from each other. You can create your own network if you can't find what you want. Expand your family of love, and live loved.

Chapter 5

Becoming Someone Else

"In order to achieve something you have never achieved before, you must become someone you have never been before."
—Albert Einstein

This chapter is about building a new daily routine to help you find your footing and give you clarity on your new path. It is filled with practical, mission-guided steps to help you realize your dreams and vision. I encourage you to have big dreams and a soaring mission—I certainly do, and owning a private plane is one of them—but you'll need to get there by taking one step at a time. It means developing new, positive attitudes, giving new habits time to stick, giving your best shot one day at a time, developing daily rituals that nurture you, and nurturing your energy for the long-haul.

When I first came across Einstein's quote, I pondered it for a while. What did it mean for me to become someone new? Would I lose my sense of identity to the point I no longer know who I am or that I even exist? What needed to be changed—what was the "new" that I would have to call in or cultivate from within? Where was I stuck or unsure, and what was I unhappy about? What new strengths did I have to develop? What kind of impact did I want to have, and how did I want to be remembered?

I recognized that the old me—habits, attitudes, beliefs, etc.—had led me to the point where I needed to start over. I desired to start over. I learned to embrace change; I tweaked and adjusted what didn't work well, and patted myself on the back when it did. I asked the big questions: "What did success mean to me? What kind of impact did I want to create? What was my purpose and my why?" The answers came to me—not all at once, but in bits and pieces. Each time I had a revelation, I added it to my tool kit. I realized that I needed a supportive daily routine, an infrastructure blending business-building activities and time-out rituals, to access inner guidance and clarify the necessary next steps.

Here are some resources that I have developed. They are tips and exercises to help you develop ways of structuring your day so that you can step up and rise up to your best self and your best life.

Habits—What to Have and What to Discard

Set the tone for the day with a ritual of gratitude. The best time to do this is in the morning. You know, the moment when you are almost awake but still a little sleepy? That is the time when your logical mind is still asleep and when your subconscious is open, making it the best time to program the mind to set the tone for the day and manifest naturally.

Use this time to go through your successes of yesterday, and affirm that you'll have a fabulous, productive day ahead, and you'll cope with any stresses or problems with awareness, ease, and faith.

Don't make your first act in the morning the mistake of grabbing your phone and scrolling through emails, news, or your social media feed. This time is for you to create what you want for yourself, not to be assaulted by outside stimuli.

Choose to define your day by what you love, and use the morning for productive me-time. I am proactive about using every minute of my morning to lay the tracks for the rest of my day. The first thing I do every morning is to look with intention at the list, in my private bathroom, of the daily activities. The list includes the little rituals I do, like affirmations, journaling, Bible scripture readings and prayers that keep me going throughout the day. This way, by looking at them first thing in the morning, they will be reinforced in my subconscious for a successful day.

I love going for a walk in the morning with my dog, and I will often listen to inspirational podcasts, strengthening prayers, or motivational talks to lend a lift to my step and put me in the right frame of mind for the day.

How long does it take to build a new habit? There are all sorts of hypotheses and theories, but the common belief is that it takes 30 days. But more recent research and studies suggest that it can take as much as 66 days for a new habit to become automatic. With that in mind, understand that you need to give yourself time to implement a new beneficial habit.

I don't believe in waiting until the end of the year to form new resolutions. If I need to consciously change, I do it now, and not wait and put my life on hold.

The Power of "I Am"

When someone asks you how you're doing, what do you say? I always reply with conviction that I'm doing well. I never say that I'm tired, because I don't wish for that thought to whisk through my mind and sap my energy level, or the one I am talking to.

There is power in the words you use: the words you use to describe and to declare who you are and how you are. It's a common default for many of you to say that you are tired, stressed, or overwhelmed, without understanding that you are reinforcing being anxious and tired. Isn't it the case that when you come across someone who keeps complaining that they are stressed, you feel your own energy draining? What if you are hammering the negative states of being into your own sub-consciousness? The most powerful words are the words you say to yourself, day in and day out.

Here is a simple thought experiment: Next time you want to blurt out "I am tired," say instead, "I am energized." Instead of saying "I am overwhelmed," offer "I'm going with the flow." It's so simple, but with each purposeful "I am" statement, you are empowering yourself with the words you use, to grow in a new expanded direction. Being tired is how you feel, it is not who you are. It is better to say, "I feel sleepy," or "I feel tired," rather than make an "I am" statement that impacts your mood negatively. Speak who you want to be, to yourself, and out loud to others . . . and you will be.

Leveraging the Power of Affirmations

To achieve big goals and big dreams, you need a healthy dose of self-belief. But if you are starting over because of a failed business or a broken relationship, your self-belief may be a little thin. What can you do to rebuild your sense of self-worth to a healthy level, and how do you put the baggage of the past behind you?

There will be highs and there will be lows in this journey of starting over and moving up, so you need to train your mind to see the best in every situation that unfolds. Affirmations are one of the most powerful resources to stock up in your toolkit. I have handpicked a list of powerful affirmations on my website, www.WomenMovingUp.com, which you can download for free, print out and put to use immediately. I refresh my list to keep pace with my own growth, but I am listing some here for you to use for starters.

It's going to be a great day.

I have happy thoughts all day long.

I show gratitude to others daily.

I have a positive encounter with everyone.

I look at and meet my goals.

I'm focused on what I want.

I release all limitations.

I think better than I feel.

I'm becoming someone that is the best version of myself.

I am full of faith, hope, and love.

Opportunities are everywhere.

I have a great imagination and I dream big, which leads to even more success.

I am a very successful investor.

I am a successful author and get paid well for writing.

I manage my money wisely.

I am completely open to receiving and managing wealth.

I am a great listener.

I am aligned with the vibrations and frequencies that attract prosperity.

I attract the right people and mentors at God's divinely appointed times.

I am supported in every area of my life.

I am creating a legacy that will bless God and others forever.

Don't be a shrinking violet when writing down the affirmations for your use every day. Be bold and be willing to challenge yourself; even be preposterous—don't short-circuit your dreams by worrying they will never happen.

I recently had a big thought, and I added it as an affirmation to my list:

I can take a company public. (This means listing a private company on the stock exchange by selling a percentage of the firm to public shareholders.)

Speak your affirmations out loud at least once a day. You can say them to yourself in the mirror. You don't have to feel like you believe them; the act of affirming is what will help you to believe and become what you are saying.

Define Your Big Why

The late great entrepreneur, author, and motivational speaker, Jim Rohn, said, *"The bigger the 'why,' the easier the 'how.'"*

Think on that for a minute to figure out what this really means to you on this part of your journey of either starting over or moving up.

The "why" refers to whether you know why you are desiring the change you are seeking. Are you aware of the reasons that are compelling this redo? Is it just for money, or is there a bigger reason? When the reason becomes clear to you, it illuminates your determination and it cements the greater purpose for your life. Without a compelling reason or "why," you won't have the burning desire and the unstoppable motivation, without which you'll be tempted to throw in the towel when the going gets tough. Take some time to clarify your why—it'll be time well spent. Come from a place of joy and purpose, not fear or pain or suffering.

Here is my example: Why am I writing this book?

Firstly, I am doing it to show my children and grandchildren that if I can author a book, they can do it too. I sought to do something I have never done before, to leave them with the understanding and the belief that there are no limitations to what they can do.

Secondly, a book expands my reach and my impact. It's like cloning myself multiple times; it is a powerful way for me to share. There are limits to physical interaction, but a book works 24/7 around the world, and there's no expiration date on it. I love being able to help people, and this book is my legacy, to inspire them and to empower them to create the life *they want*—not a life they think they should have, but the one they truly desire with every fiber of their being.

Have a Greater Purpose

It's one of life's biggest questions: What's your purpose in life? What is calling you, and what are you contributing to the world? Some refer to this as a calling. I prefer to say callings, because there can be more than one over a person's lifetime.

Your purpose is your compass through life; it moves you in the direction you need to go, it gives you confidence, it stirs your passion, and it rouses you to take action. It's a question everyone needs to answer, and for someone starting over like you are, you need to prioritize this. Without this compass, your next steps are unclear, and you may end up dashing around willy-nilly, wasting time and energy in the process.

This is a gift you need to give yourself: the time to think through what your life purpose is, to dream and journal about it, and to talk to someone about it. The more you direct your attention to finding your answer, the more clarity will bubble up.

I do believe that there is a season for everything, and your life purpose may change. When my children were growing up, my one purpose was to take care of them and raise them well. Now they have their own children, and I am working hard to be a support to them—not like a helicopter mom, but as someone who will encourage them to reach for their best, and someone they can look up to, be inspired by, and be comforted by.

My purpose now is different. It is to help women, like you, navigate the process of starting over, with ease and success. I have done it and so can you. I am passing along my experiences with moving up my money thermostat to bring in more financial success, so that you can realize your own dreams, and help other women in turn.

I have a greater, overriding purpose: to build and sustain a love relationship with God, and with other people. This is a lesson we all need to learn; if everyone learns to love each other, we won't have the current problems that are crippling our societies. We won't have racism, where we demonize another and think them inferior; we won't have social inequality, hunger, or wars, and we won't have gender discrimination.

In defining your purpose, be mindful that it needs to have a broad focus, and not just be focused on details like making more money. Of course, having more money is necessary, but as you are writing out your purpose, take a step back and think bigger. Your purpose is your fuel. It gives you clear-mindedness and shapes every step you take, from short-term tasks to long-term goals. It may seem like a lot of work. But there is a part in you—and in everyone—that knows there is a purpose to being alive, even if that understanding is currently blanketed by confusion and anxiety. Once you get in touch with the inner knowing, you'll find that your purpose gives meaning to your life and it sets you on fire. You will no longer just be going through the motions or drifting through life; you'll be living a purpose-driven life. If you are struggling with knowing your purpose, the book *The Purpose Driven Life: What on Earth Am I Here For?* by Rick Warren has sold tens of millions of copies all over the world and is well worth reading.

Draw up a Dream List

In order to turn what you want into reality, you need to draw up a dream list. You need this list to embolden you, to get you to where you want to go, and to get you what you really want out of life. Some of you dream of wooing the world with acting skills;

others are born to be musicians to arouse feelings with music. And there are some of you who dream of being entrepreneurs to solve problems and meet needs, while creating economic opportunity and growth for the communities you impact.

At the same time, while you may have lofty dreams, there may be others, like wanting to travel or learn to speak several languages, be a better cook, or a more patient gardener, and in my case, be an author. Don't waste your life fulfilling someone else's dreams for you. Whatever makes it to your list, don't short-change yourself. Dream big and dream bigger yet again.

I have had it on my list to write a book and to start a podcast, both of which I have now done. Check. I also want to own a private plane so that I can be free to travel whenever I want to; be able to see my kids more often, and take them on vacations to fun places; and leverage my ability to find business opportunities.

Dreaming can be new for you, as it was for me. I had to practice how to dream about life, and I had to give myself permission to dare to dream. In many ways, I lived to achieve other people's expectations. But then I decided I needed to dream purposefully and to take time out to dream. The question that helped me was that if time and money were not an issue, what would I want to do with my life?

> **Here's a tip:** Next to each of your dreams, write out your reason why. Next to my dreams to be an author and podcaster, I wrote down that they widen my reach and help me influence many more people, because I love to help others, especially brave women like you who are starting over and moving up.

A piece of advice: Be diligent about including in your dream list how much money and passive income you want to have. Passive income is defined as income that requires little to no effort to earn and maintain (because you've already done all the hard work). It is income earned while you sleep, so to speak, and is derived from sources like royalties, rentals, interest on bonds, and dividends from your stocks, amongst others.

It's a good goal to aim high, and you can break it down into various time frames: a five-year goal, a three-year goal, a one-year goal, a monthly goal, and a weekly goal. I am not going to expound on goal setting here; there are plenty of resources available to go deeper if you want.

Here are some other fun tools you can include in the toolkit to realize your dreams:

Vision Board: I have a vision board in my office, on which I have photos of beautiful clothing because, some day, I would like to design clothes. I have included inspiring words like, "Spring Forward," I cut out from magazines, a bench for the joy of reflection, and someone boarding a private jet for travel. There is a picture of a walk-in closet, one that is bigger and more modern than the one I currently have.

I have pinned on the vision board ribbons of awards that I have won for public speaking. It's a reinforcement of my successes, and an affirmation that, yes, I have more awards coming. Put on your vision board every accomplishment you seek, and every desire you want fulfilled. Use photos or pictures, or even quotes, to visually represent your dreams.

Imagining: It is really simple. Exercise your God-given imagination gift. Set aside a few minutes a day—preferably when you are most relaxed, such as when you first wake up or right before you sleep—after your meditation or your prayers. You sit comfortably, close your eyes and, in your mind, imagine in as great detail as you can, what it is that you wish to manifest. Add some "oomph" to your visualization by feeling the emotions of joy, happiness, and accomplishment that you would feel when you get to what and where you are imagining. Anchoring your visualizations in feelings effectively turbo-charges the manifestation and accelerates the achievement.

Meditating: Meditation instils calmness, reduces stress, and grounds you in present awareness. When I meditate, I turn everything off—TV, phone, my mental chatter—for 20 minutes. I breathe deeply to relax into the moment and to center myself, and I meditate on verses from the Bible, those that comfort or strengthen me. There are other meditation techniques; focusing on your in and out breathing is one. Find one that works for you, because meditation is a great way to restore your inner being, and to revitalize and renew your energy in the middle of a stressful or hectic day.

Cut Yourself Some Slack: Wherever you are starting over from, you know it's not going to be a straightforward journey. There will be detours, dead ends, and delays, and you'll make mistakes. This is no time to be a perfectionist—anyway, perfectionism is over-rated and is boring. Instead by being willing to live with your mistakes, you are able to reposition yourself and recognize the opportunities that surround you.

I keep a journal close to me, to write down a frustration or to get something off my mind. Or I speak whatever I am vexed about into a recorder to blow off some steam. Often, I'll rewind the recording and listen to myself, and I'll feel better for getting it off my chest.

So, cut yourself some slack; God does. He gives us grace when we are learning; why don't you do the same for yourself?

Believing in Your Self-Worth

If there's only one thing you take away from this chapter, take this:

You are worth it!

You are worth every cent you wish to earn, every dream you want to realize. And you have to be your own best cheerleader, because if you don't believe in yourself, who will? We're all vulnerable to the mind chatter that says we aren't worth it, but if you smother your sense of self-worth, you are giving self-doubt the upper hand. The result is that it will smother your dreams.

You are the person you believe yourself to be. Use the time you've been given wisely, and be the person you want to be. Others are waiting for what you can do to make the world a more loving and abundant place.

Success Story from Kim Mladenov to Nora Ellen

Before my husband and I started We Care Dental, LLC. in Phoenix, AZ, I could never understand the challenge of owning a business . . . a business you rely on to provide for your family . . . a business that makes you work harder than you've ever worked just to pay your employees, sometimes not being able to pay yourselves . . . and a business that has stretched us to believe when we felt like we were sinking. From day one, Nora has championed us.

In addition to offering great advice and mentoring, she became our patient, which provided her the opportunity to offer her unique perspective and feedback.

Nora's coaching continues to be strategic and very beneficial as we work to grow our business. Time and time again Nora will reach out to ask how our business is going and to offer inspiration and motivation. More than any other friend, Nora's words have been creative and laser-focused, targeting the practical aspects of entrepreneurship like marketing and outreach.

We are so grateful for Nora's love and investment in us. In spite of the challenges and the great likelihood that we would fail, as so many new businesses do, we just celebrated our 5th anniversary. We give all glory to God! Through His grace, hard work and thanks to wonderful coaching with Nora, we are still here and we are excited to see what the future holds. - Kim Mladenov, Owner of We Care Dental, LLC in Phoenix, AZ. www.wecaredentalaz.com

Chapter 6

The 9 Pinnacles of Power

*"When you stop chasing the wrong things,
you give the right things a chance to catch you."*
—Lolly Daskal

Not too long ago, I had the joy of being a speaker at a runner's club, and I spoke about *The 9 Pinnacles of Power* that aid you in starting over. Think of them as touchstones of power that you can draw upon to remove self-imposed barriers, and to help you shift to step into the larger life that's calling you. You'll notice that two of these pinnacles—enthusiasm and determination—are covered in greater detail because they are necessary to helping you get out of "stuckness," unlock your own extraordinary potential, and create the big changes you desire in your life.

Power of Clarity

I was at a business meeting once when the speaker said something that resonated with me, about our gifts and callings and how being a business owner was much more than just selling; there was a calling to it. I went up to him (I was a real estate agent then) and asked how I could make being a realtor a calling. But it was more about how I could make a calling a living. He said that clarity is power, and it got me thinking: What do I want? What kind of person do I want to be? How do I want to be remembered?

Writing down goals is a great idea; it brings clarity that helps to illuminate your journey forward, like a car's headlights cutting through fog. Recently, I was feeling overwhelmed, so I wrote down on a board all the tasks I needed to do. I liked having everything up on the board—ideas, tools, marketing strategies, possible partnerships, etc.—because I remembered and focused better when I wrote things down. Having the big picture view in front of me gave me strength to believe that I could do it. With clarity, I am more intentional about my next steps to help more people make more money.

When you tap into the *power of clarity*, your vision isn't drowned out by the fear and anxieties of the collective. Even in current uncertain and chaotic conditions, you'll understand what's happening, cut through the flak, create opportunities that would otherwise not exist, and achieve financial success under any economic condition.

Power of Proximity

Be close to people and groups of people whom you want to be like, and whom you admire and appreciate. I hope you're benefitting from the support of good mentors, and are in turn mentoring others. There are regional mastermind groups, as well as national and international ones, that conduct their meetings in online chat rooms. Who are the people that form your support system? How do you network with people? Are you meeting with people who are already successful in your chosen profession, and from whom you'll learn exponentially? Are you meeting up with people who admire you, or with those who challenge you?

We become like the people we spend our time with. Consciously choose the people you meet and mingle with. Make a list of your current communities and social networks. From that list, make one of your "25 dream people"—successful entrepreneurs, thought leaders, elected officials, authors, charity volunteers, church leaders, professors, motivational speakers—with whom you want to work and collaborate. In this group you can include your family, people you come across, and those people who inspire and motivate you, and in whose footsteps you aim to follow. You might be surprised at how fast your list can grow, and the mutual benefit. If you find you came up short, then consider increasing or changing your social networks.

We hear more and more that your income is linked to the people whom you hang out with. Don't fall for the myth that all rich people are odious; I personally know multi-millionaires and billionaires that are very giving and generous and are willing to help. You'll find as you read this book that I am a myth breaker and will help you break off old thinking that does not serve you, or anyone, for that matter.

Power of Purity

I didn't really think of purity as power until recently. We want purity in our nutrition and be purely devoted in our relationships. We want pure water and pure organic food, and a pure mind, and we avoid junk food. That applies to what we put into our minds. On social media, I find a lot of trolling and name-calling, which adds little to my mindset other than dragging me down.

I would encourage you to actively be conscious of what you are listening to and watching, and the people you are mingling with. Are your activities, entertainment and relationships supporting you or making you dissatisfied with your own life? Are they uplifting and rewarding, or dragging you down to the level of the under-achiever and the ordinary?

I am not big on film and television, as many of their entertainment values don't quite sync with mine. I believe we are much more impacted by the entertainment we consume than we may ever know. Plus, I want to be so busy enjoying my own life and adventures rather than plopping down to watch TV which doesn't really enhance my life or make me a better person in this mission I am on. And, so much entertainment oversexualizes us women. Too much TV, film and music overly portrays us as sex-crazed machines and has seemed to program some of us to be this way. We're depicted as the ones who are to be the pursuer, the seductress, the one to make the first move. Don't buy that as the norm. Most of this kind of entertainment is produced by men who too often exploit women sexually. There are many single women who believe in the benefits of sexual purity, as I do, and are unapologetic with this lifestyle. The advantages of abstinence, are being free of worry of sexually transmitted diseases, getting pregnant, or having our emotions tripped up over a man we think we have to prove ourselves to. We are wired to be emotionally impacted by sexual relations, and much entertainment does not show the reality of the effect of being sexually active or promiscuous outside of marriage. Respect yourself. You will only be respected by others to the degree that you respect yourself. Make sure what goes into your body, soul and spirit is pure so you can move forward in a greater fulfilling and longer lasting way.

In one of the sitcoms I used to watch, I noticed that the kids in the sitcom were joking a lot about sex. I became uncomfortable about a script and a show where children actors were given lines by adults, which focused so much on sex. Then there are the children watching these shows learning about sex as if it's the norm. How are they then to know if someone is touching them inappropriately when sex is portrayed as fun and humorous? That didn't work for me, especially since the evils of sex trafficking are so prolific, and this kind of joking is confusing for children in their relationships with adults. I stopped watching immediately because I do not want to be a consumer that adds to this wrongdoing; I want to be part of the solution to protect our children. Don't fill up your mind and dull it with trashy entertainment.

We become what we consume, whether it's the food we eat, what we drink, the entertainment we enjoy, the social media we utilize and so forth. So much can be self-focused and life draining. Choose the *power of purity* to help be who you want to be and what you want to be about in an impure and hurting world.

Power of Enthusiasm

Enthusiasm is infectious. There's something charming and appealing about someone who is upbeat, eager, and dynamic, and has a passion and a zeal for a hobby, a cause, or a profession. But is enthusiasm wired into a woman's DNA or personality, or is it a cultivated trait that comes out of having an intense and purposeful focus?

I say that enthusiasm is a felt sense that can be self-generated, but it can also be willed into being with self-discipline. When

I need to raise my energy for an appointment that I am not looking forward to or am apprehensive about, I do this little ritual: I look in the mirror, turn on a big smile, look excited, and raise my energy level by saying to my reflection, "This is so exciting! Great, terrific, awesome. I'm so fortunate; this is the best appointment ever, and I will achieve success." Doing this ups my energy level, and I will go to the appointment in a great mood—enthusiasm is contagious; it rubs off on the people I am meeting.

In her book *Miracles Happen*, Mary Kay Ash insists that her beauty consultants do not turn on the hard sell during their presentations, but instead focus on being enthusiastic about the products because they sincerely believe in them. That's the better way because enthusiasm is a trait you can integrate into your life and practice every day.

Enthusiasm is not fake, nor is it insincere. You need to do whatever you have to in order to get the *power of enthusiasm* surging through your veins. It's not a lie to act enthusiastic, because when you do, you will become enthused. When you do this enough, the energy creates its own momentum, which moves you forward smoothly. No one is enthusiastic 24/7, and that's the truth. There are days when you feel you just don't have it within you, and that's okay. Nonetheless, if there's a challenge you have to face, there are little daily rituals that help you recharge this particular power of enthusiasm.

Ways to create enthusiasm:

- **Tap into self-discipline.** When enthusiasm wanes because you have taken on too much and you don't quite get to the finish line, drop into your self-discipline and take one small step, because small steps can change everything in the long run. For example, I was stuck at the third chapter of a book and stopped reading it for a while. I decided that it was worth trying again, to read maybe just one more chapter, and in no time, I finished the whole book and greatly benefitted from its motivational stories and tips.

- **Enthusiasm stems from a burning desire.** When you have a burning desire, something remarkable happens. When you want it so badly that nothing else matters, the desire sharpens your mind and stimulates your imagination, and you become more alert to potential opportunities that help you fulfill that desire.

- **Enthusiasm doesn't have to be showy.** It can have its own quiet strength. Henry Ford was known to be a low-key person, with a monotonous speech. He was not a larger-than-life figure, but his enthusiasm about his inventions stirred up his imagination, strengthened his faith, and won people over to his side. He thought in his mind what he would accomplish, and he sought out to get it done because he viewed enthusiasm as "the irresistible surge of will and energy to execute your ideas."

- **Visualize the prize on the other side.** When enthusiasm wanes, picture what is waiting for you: a sense of accomplishment, the satisfaction of improving yourself, or helping someone get or achieve something that will improve their lives.

I wish to draw the line between over-enthusiasm that is rooted in the wrong motivation, and genuine enthusiasm. An overloud, overbearing, over-enthusiastic person comes across as being fake. In fact, it's a form of manipulation: using that kind of energy to bend another person to his or her will. Genuine enthusiasm doesn't seek to control another; it just *is*, and it lets the other person make up their mind.

Let me leave you with these words by Ralph Waldo Emerson. He said, *"Nothing great was achieved without enthusiasm."*

Power of Determination

Determination is like a magic key that will unlock doors to your success. With determination, you have the unwavering belief that it's going to work—you are singularly focused, no one can change your mind, and no one can dissuade you otherwise. And you keep going and going and going, until you prove yourself or achieve your goal. Determination is a powerful emotion. It's a kind of stubbornness that is strengthening and empowering. It's also enjoyable because, when it is running in full force, it fuels you, and you feel you can conquer mountains. The greater your determination, the greater the reward you reap.

Determination is the opposite of passivity; it staves off mediocrity and helps you over hump days and stumbling blocks. Determination shapes what you do every day. Each time you pass over the opportunity to take a step toward your dreams, is you effectively saying that your dreams aren't worth it. But with determination, you have a higher purpose, and the more determined you are, the more people will buy into your purpose and motivation.

This is a good time to bring up the naysayers: the ones who tell you that your goals and dreams won't work. I call these people "crabs in a basket." Have you ever noticed, when you have a mass of crabs in a basket, when one tries to get out, the other crabs pull it back into the basket? Such people want to drag you down to their level because they don't want to be left behind when you fly high. If you want to be extraordinary, you won't get there by hanging out with those who hold you back, because you'll stay as ordinary as they are.

I am determined to use my time wisely, to accomplish everything I need to do in order to get to where I want to be, in terms of financial success and freedom. As you are starting over or moving up, determine what you want by way of financial freedom; put on blinders like those worn by a horse, and see only the way ahead of you. Keep telling yourself, "I've got to do this. I am determined."

When I was a young mother in my 20s, I decided to sell Avon because it was the one thing I could do with children at home. In those days, an Avon representative could only work in a designated territory. Determined to get started, I called the director of the territory I wanted, every hour, and left messages until she called back. When I was starting out, I was determined to be the best Avon representative in my region and, despite being nervous, I decided to knock on every door. I hung a catalog with a sample on each door in my territory, and went back later to introduce myself. Giving something of value away is crucial to building a relationship of trust. In this way, I built a pretty good client list, and about five of them became like a "golden goose" for my business. It meant that each of their orders netted me thousands of dollars over time, which was pretty good for working part time.

It was the same when I moved on to selling real estate, when I first started back during the Great Recession of 2008. I sent out an announcement that I was now selling real estate, hoping I would get some clients. Nothing happened. In my determination, I started studying what successful agents did and came up with other activities that paid off, bringing me to earning a six-figure income. Determination gets you to where your goal is.

Power of Authority

What does the word "authority" bring up in you? On dictionary.com, authority is defined as "the power to determine, adjudicate, or otherwise settle issues or disputes. It's having a jurisdiction, the right to control, command, or determine. It's a power or right, delegated or given. It's a person or body of persons in whom authority is vested, as a governmental agency."

Authority is there to protect, guide, and be helpful. I must acknowledge that some people have sadly misused and abused their power of authority, such as teachers, religious leaders, scout leaders, law enforcement, and relatives that have abused children. That is absolutely the wrong use of power, and should be exposed as such and dealt with.

In this day and age, there is greater dissent against authority because many feel betrayed and hurt, but I wish to highlight the plus side of being an authority.

I am an authority on what I am writing about, and I hope it will greatly benefit you in many ways. My ideas and suggestions are lessons derived from my successes and mistakes. By sharing them with you, I hope you can avoid the common pitfalls of starting over, and move up the success curve more quickly than I did.

People refer to authorities for their expertise and experience, because the authority has insights and knowledge that the people need. This brings me to you and this power. In which field of expertise are you an authority, and how can you leverage that to earn income?

Here's a tip: Write a book. You're probably saying right now that you can't do that, but if all the authors in the world thought that, we wouldn't have libraries, nor would we have the luxury of learning from or escaping into a good book. A book is a great legacy to leave.

You can write on any subject matter that sings to you, and in which you have expertise, be it fiction, non-fiction, or biographies, or your own memoirs to leave behind for the people in your family who come after you.

I didn't think to ask my parents much about their lives until I was much older, and now I wish I had pressed them for more details, or that they had written down some memoirs that I could share with my children, and they with their children. My father fought in World War II, and he sent money home to his parents to help them out of hard times. But I wish I knew more: How was it in the front lines? Was life harsh then? From little anecdotes and bits and pieces, I realized my dad was very thoughtful and caring about others, but I don't know a whole lot more. I know more about my mother's life, and I was able to learn from her mistakes; that meant a lot to me.

A person may have book learning and paper credentials but lack the ability to use the know-how in a manner that benefits others.

That is not an authority. In my definition, it's someone who has the understanding, the wisdom, and the ability to translate the knowledge to positively impact others. A person doesn't need titles to be an authority; anyone who is a natural leader is someone who will command the respect and following of others.

Author, speaker, and pastor, John C. Maxwell, is one of the world's best in training others to be leaders, and he has grown into his power over time; so much so, he's seen as the authority in the field of leadership. In his advanced certification courses, he draws on 45 years of leadership and influence to teach the principles of entrepreneurship, speaking, selling, coaching, leadership, and mindset for success.

What have you done and how would you like to show you are an authority in your field?

Power of Humor

Humor delights; it makes people feel good, it defuses confrontation, and a good laugh gets rid of stress immediately. Remember the last time you laughed so much your sides ached? That's the gift of humor. Humor cuts across racial, age, and cultural lines, and builds connections. I was once in a park and walked by a group of people speaking an unknown language. They suddenly burst into laughter, and while I didn't understand what brought it on, I had a good chuckle myself, and then realized humor and laughter is the most internationally understood language.

I work on intentionally making people laugh, but I don't use sarcasm. To me, sarcasm is not humor; it's actually a form of self-defense, can be abusive and is not universally appreciated.

Laughter is infectious, it's fun, and it changes our mood and our body chemistry. It's a great way to pivot from the negative to the positive.

I was once with two friends, driving through a beautiful forest with evergreen trees and tall pines. However, instead of enjoying the scenery, my friends were busy talking about their problems. Getting tired of the negativity, I thought about some funny thing I could say to change the tone, then butted in and said, "Look at all of those future Christmas trees." Somehow that got all of us laughing, and the conversation moved into a more upbeat, cheerful tone, which allowed us to enjoy the rest of the afternoon.

Humor can boost information retention, and a good teacher or preacher makes good use of it. A study of 400 college students, on student learning and instructional humor theory, showed that appropriate humor from their teachers increased retention of their classroom lessons, while cruel or unrelated humor did not.

I laugh at myself frequently. I laugh when I overcook my food, or take a wrong turn or dial an incorrect number. I laugh at my mistakes, but I do not laugh at others or their problems. I get along best with people who are able to laugh at themselves, and I have found that humor got me going when I made mistakes, because it helped me to easily flip the switch. You've heard people say, "Don't take yourself too seriously," and I agree!

When the going gets tough, laugh. When the going gets good, become a story-teller that makes people laugh, because that's how you build connections and spread your influence.

Power of Joy

Joy is different from happiness. I find that feelings of happiness are more fleeting: They come and go in a moment's notice; they appear and disappear like vapor, and they are not emotions we have control over. There is a lot of literature and discussion on happiness and why it is important for success, and why it is so pivotal for people to be happy. As a result of so much emphasis being placed on happiness in the cultural mindset, you find large swaths of people desiring happiness and pursuing happiness as if it was the only goal that matters.

I choose to pursue joy in my life. Joy is more enduring; it sinks more deeply into your soul, and it comes from emotional maturity. Joy is rooted in knowing who you are, understanding your purpose in life, and enjoying more contentment and peace. Joy is more about appreciating your life and staying confident and at peace, even when life throws a temper tantrum or a few wobbles along your path, and happiness seems elusive at that point in time.

I find that there are people who think there is something wrong with them if they are not happy, and they seek to try different jobs and experiences, and switch in and out of relationships, hoping something new will make them happy. So they are always chasing something elusive, and the failure to catch that moving object, sends them into depression.

I think that depression can sometimes be caused by a lack of joy and contentment in a person's life, and having expectations that may not match what they are capable of achieving. For such a person, the focus is on feeling what I describe as the drug-like high of happiness from fleeting wins or owning material comforts, rather than focusing on purpose and meaning that brings about a lifetime of joy, satisfaction, and contentment.

When I went through divorce and painful disappointments in my life, I was not very happy. In fact, I was very unhappy, and I grieved the loss of that dream. Yet I still had joy in my life. My joy was, and still is, derived from spirituality and my close relationship with God and His presence, which is the meaning in my life.

I believe that joy can be a huge preventive and an antidote to depression.

For example, I experienced a lot of joy in sponsoring an underprivileged child through Compassion International, www.Compassion.com. This charity describes joy as:

". . . an attitude of the heart and spirit, present inside of us as an untapped reservoir of potential.

It's possible to feel joy in difficult times. Joy doesn't need a smile in order to exist, although it does feels better with one. Joy can share its space with other emotions: sadness, shame, or anger. Happiness can't.

Happiness is not present in darkness and difficulty. Joy never leaves it. Joy undergirds our spirits; it brings to life, peace and contentment.

Joy requires a connection. Often, the connection is with other people, but it can also be with pets, creation, creativity, etc. Joy is present. In the moment. Happiness mostly just passes through.

With joy, there is hope. With joy, hardship offers growth and opportunity. With joy, self-esteem and self-respect are indestructible."

Instead of making happiness your goal and focus, aim for joy!

Power of Love

What does love mean to you? Does it refer to your husband, your kids, your dog, cat, house, chocolate, movies, or vacation? I don't think we have enough words in the English language to fully express the various shades and nuances of love. We say we love ice cream, we love our boyfriend, we love our new shoes, and we love a movie. But the emotion, even though we are using the same word, is vastly different in those circumstances. The Greeks have words to describe different kinds of love. For example, Eros is for romantic or passionate love, and Philia is for friendship or brotherly love (Philia is the Greek root word for Philadelphia, the City of Brotherly Love). Agape has to do with perfect love, the kind God has for us. Xenia is a type of friendship or hospitality, and the love of serving others.

Love is extremely powerful. We all want to be loved, wanted, desired, appreciated, honored, and respected. Those who feel and live loved, and those who are able to give love, are some of the happiest and most joyful people I know. When people feel unloved, unwanted, and lonely, it saps their life force and strength, and they can turn into victims, sometimes wanting to hide away or lash out at others.

I am not talking about romantic love in this chapter; it's the kind of love more along the lines of Xenia and Philia. This is the definition of love that I appreciate most, and it comes from the love chapter, (1 Corinthians 13), in the Bible: *Love is patient, love is kind. It is not jealous or envious; it is not proud or boastful; it is not selfish or rude. It always trusts, always hopes, is not easily angered, or delights in evil, but celebrates the truth. It always protects, trusts, and perseveres. Love never fails.*

When you start over and treat others (as well as yourself) with love and compassion, you will succeed. Be that kind of a person who will support others, be willing to fight for them, think the best of them, and put their interests before your own. You will naturally draw people to you, because this kind of love builds connections that offer value, sustenance, and compassion. No one wants to hire an unloving, uncaring consultant, or a disgruntled, uninterested employee. No one wants to buy a product without care being put into the transaction.

Love and care have to be put into every effort, to be successful financially. By making love my priority in my service to my clients, I have enjoyed repeated successes in real estate and other income-producing businesses. I encourage you to do the same, to be a stand out in this challenging and oftentimes loveless world.

I believe that no greater truth has ever been spoken than in the Bible, *"Love never fails."*

Fun Exercise

Pick 3 pinnacles of power that you would like to live out loud. For each, jot down how you achieved success in these areas, and include a past story of similar success. Reliving your achievements, and imprinting them more fully in your awareness, gives you motivation to go out and do even more.

Choose 2 of the 9 power pinnacles that you would like to strengthen. Write out the benefits that will accrue to you from leveraging each of these power pinnacles more strongly.

Share your thoughts with friends who have committed to be supportive of you in this journey. Do this over coffee or tea, and be sure to find something to laugh about. There is a sense of self-empowerment that you'll gain when you openly speak about this to a friend—and who better to hold you accountable than someone with whom you have a close connection.

Chapter 7

The Help You Don't Know You Have

"Twenty years from now, you will be more disappointed by the things that you didn't do than by the ones you did do. So throw off the bowlines. Sail away from the safe harbor. Catch the trade winds in your sails. Explore. Dream. Discover."
—H. Jackson Brown, Jr.

You're not alone in your journey of starting over and moving up, even if you may feel that you are. You may feel overwhelmed or knocked down because there is so much that is unknown before you. Whether you are starting over, deliberately beginning anew, or seeking to move up in the world, you are facing a major life shift.

But don't give up. There are a lot of people waiting to help you, in the very same way that you've helped others. Technology has moved the goal posts for us in this new normal. This is the age of information and knowledge, and with tools available to us at the tap of a finger, it's now easier for us to launch a new business, connect with people, acquire new skills, and extend our reach to other communities.

It has also made it possible to find your tribe, the like-minded people with whom you resonate and who will help and support you move toward your vision. If you don't give up in the face of such an incredible shift in your life, I assure you that there will come a time when you will look back at this time with fondness. You'll be grateful you chose to forge through this season of growth, and you'll remember it as that special time of your life:

- When you found you were bigger than your problems.
- When you came to fully understand your purpose in life.
- When you were given the opportunity to discard the old ways that no longer work for you.
- When you were placed at a nexus in time to find new possibilities to grow and change.
- When you overcame old self-limiting ways to become a more powerful manifestor and creator of possibilities for others.

Don't run away from your problems; this is the time to grow yourself, to be bigger than your problems, and to focus on opportunity. So how do you reset your life, and where do you find the help you need?

Where Do You Start?

This is likely a time of financial hardship, so start with getting help in this area so that you can buy food and pay pressing bills.

There are non-profit organizations, churches, and charities that are set up to help women make transitions. This may be a tough pill to swallow for those of us who have never asked for help, or you may find that you really need the financial support in order to take the next steps. Look close to home, at city, state, or federal aid, or charities that benefit women. Don't let pride stand in your way.

Through my podcasts, I have come across three wonderful women who have reinvented themselves successfully, but all three of them lived on welfare for a time because it was exactly what they needed to get through financial stress. One of them was a single mother who was going through college, and she needed the aid to finish her degree and bring up her child.

Help Is on the Other Side of a Relationship

I have always known that help is on the other side of a relationship. This is the time in your life when you need to connect with people, and everything you need now is facilitated through the help of others. I have a list of 100 Eagles: people who have supported me, people I admire and respect and who love me, and people I want to learn from or want most to be like. Among these smart and driven people, I have my children (even my grandkids, because I derive so much joy from them), my best clients, mentors (and even people I want to be mentored by), a favorite author, the city mayor, my pastor, a charity director and an internet influencer—all of them are people I can learn from. These are the people I want to be close to, and whom I feel will be in my corner cheering me on when I run out of steam.

Here's a tip: Put together your list of 100 Eagles right now. These are the people you need most right now, and you may be surprised how quickly you get to 100. Start with less Eagles, if you feel 100 is too daunting a number, and include the ones who bring joy and positivity into your life, and those with whom you had meaningful work relationships.

It may even be the boss who fired you, or the manager who didn't want to lay you off, because what they did forced you to do better. It may be an old professor who encouraged you in school. These are the people who are your biggest fans, who will cheer and inspire you to want to do more, offer you ongoing encouragement, and give you the boost you need. These are the people who will lift you higher and who will help you, not hurt you.

Connecting and Networking

Someone recently told me that I had a gift for connecting people together, and for networking. I never thought of it as a gift; it just seems natural to me that if I met someone who had a need, and I knew someone else who could fulfill that need, I would put them in touch with each other. For example, if someone has a health problem that can be corrected through proper nutrition, and I happen to know a nutritionist that I respect, I would put the two together. Or I would connect two or more people who may be doing the same thing and believe in the same mission. Together, they can bounce ideas off each other and lend each other motivation to create their next steps.

The thought of networking may be unpalatable to many people. And maybe it could be because of the old, outdated thinking around networking being "pressing the flesh." I don't think of it that way. It could be that I'm a really good listener and I really like people. As such, I just don't like to attach a label to connecting with people—I prefer to think of it as helping people, of facilitating relationships, and putting together people who can help each other for a common purpose. To me, connecting with others is a way of pulling together those who can bring blessings and benefit into your life. Life can't be done any other way.

There is no shortage of business networking events that you can tap into. I always come back with something useful from every networking event I go to. If you go a few minutes early, it is easy to meet people and not have to break into groups of people who are familiar with each other. I tend to turn up early and introduce myself to the person standing alone. Such a person is always more appreciative of meeting someone willing to step out and approach them to start a conversation.

I always go with goals in mind. When you go to these meetings, be intentional. Ask how you can help people there. Many of you find it hard to break the ice with a stranger. Here is my tip: When you approach a stranger, say, "My name is so and so, and you look like an interesting person to talk to." Who wouldn't like to be told that he or she is an interesting person? Next, I ask the person, "What brought you here, or what got you into doing what you do today?" It's a more genuine conversation starter than plunging ahead with a standard "what do you do?" To make a sincere connection, be fully present and focused on the person you are with. This is not the time to be looking around the room to see who else is there, or checking your social media feed or texts, because your sincere, focused attention is the best compliment to the person you are with. Remember, they're there for the same reason you are, to meet people to be able to become more successful.

I aim to attend at least one networking function every week. There are some strictly business-oriented networking events, but there are other activities organized by the social networks or communities you are part of, such as book clubs or meet-up groups that are linked to the area of expertise you want to move into. Identify meaningful projects, where you can work with and develop valuable bonds with others. Find groups through which you'll derive benefits, such as acquiring a needed skill or filling in a knowledge gap. If growing your own food or protecting the environment is a passion, you may want to join a community garden. Be willing and ready to put yourself out there to make life-enhancing relationships and positive results that will move you forward. Check local libraries and community colleges for free courses aimed at helping women start businesses, or those who are starting afresh. I recommend checking out *Gale Courses,* which are taught by university professors and are usually free. In this information age, your knowledge and expertise are your most powerful tools.

Even if you live in a rural area or have to be in quarantine, as we have had this year, connect through online forums or meetings and such. Reach out and say what your goals are, be willing to explain why you're in this financial hardship, and ask what advice they can offer you. People appreciate a genuinely honest person. Or pick up the phone and call your 100 Eagles. When I told my 100 Eagles that they were on my list, they were surprised and delighted, and willing to help.

In a Season of Growth, Give to Others

What goes around comes around. You reap what you sow, and the scriptures say, "It's more blessed to give than to receive."

Even in a time of hardship, when you are caught between a rock and a hard place, I encourage you to give—if not of money, because you don't have enough to spare, give of your time and energy. Volunteerism is a great way to network and meet all kinds of people. Charities are always looking for help, be they women's centers, seniors' homes, pet rescue shelters, or food banks. You can give by helping out churches and ministries. You never know who you are going to meet. And when you meet people who might be able to help you, have the courage to ask for help.

There are people who will mentor you for free, or there may be times when you will have to pay for professional help, which you may need to help you get rid of self-limiting beliefs. I am a coach myself, and I pay a coach to help me, because having a different perspective, and learning from someone who is already successful in my chosen profession, is always helpful. Even rich and wealthy people have coaches.

Keep your mind fixed on helping others. Giving helps you feel better about yourself, and even if you are having a rough time, this is the best time to give. It benefits you spiritually and psychologically. The more you give away, the more you open yourself to receive. It's a law of the Universe. We are made to help someone because, without helping each other, we are all pretty much doomed.

Alternatively, if you are reading this book during a downturn in the economy, how about starting your own food drive for a particular family? You'll amaze others with your initiative and creativity. The more you rise above your own needs and problems by enriching the lives of others, the more you increase and enhance your value and the public perception of your marketability. This is important because you get paid in proportion to the value you bring to the marketplace. When you give, you reap so much. Your confidence in yourself will grow. People will see you as successful and as an authority in helping others. The more you interact with others, the faster you release limiting self-beliefs that may have gotten you into this hard situation in the first place. Giving is one way of understanding the root causes that are holding you back.

> *"No one has ever become poor by giving."*
> —Anne Frank

Big Changes Start with Small Steps

Life is a journey made in small steps. You need to move forward because, if you don't, you'll always stay in the same place, and that's not what starting over is about. Even when the going is tough and you find you need to dig more deeply into your inner resources, it's crucial that you take the necessary small steps every day. Here, I've outlined a few for you to include in your process of starting over.

As you are making significant changes in your life, there may come a time when you will wonder if you may need to go back to school to acquire missing skills. Are paper credentials always necessary, or can you self-educate and learn on the job?

I have 4 years of college, but I do not have a degree. I was not motivated to graduate with a degree, because when I worked during the summers, alongside college graduates, I discovered that I made as much money as they did. After my 4th year of college, I earned more money than college graduates, even those with a post graduate degree. I say that the best education is "caught," not "taught." In years past, there would be apprentice programs; if there's something you want to go in to, find someone who will allow you to shadow them, be it someone who teaches you how to get into the bakery or the construction business, or into any profession that you wish. There are many ways to bring income and without having a college degree.

Don't overlook tapping into temporary agencies to find you part-time work that will help you pay the bills until you land on your feet. Or you may consider working with a head-hunter to help you become more competitive in your job search. Recruiters are more in touch with changing market conditions, and they may pinpoint new areas of need that you may not know about.

Just because you are starting over doesn't mean you are lacking in skills. You have certain work experiences and expertise that you can immediately leverage. In the gig economy, temporary positions are common, as companies hire short-term workers for short-term commitments or for specific projects. There are online freelance marketing services that post jobs, or where you can offer your services and bid for jobs. You just never know—what may start as part-time work, may end up being your next full time profession.

At this point in your journey, I also highly recommend pairing up with an accountability partner. This is someone you want to be accountable to; for example, in two important areas, such as networking or goal-setting. If you are an introvert, you may suffer from "call reluctance," and you'll need to account to your partner for the calls you've made. On the other hand, if you are an extrovert, you may need accountability in other areas, such as effective listening, to help you process information that will influence your future direction.

Part of effective accountability is a practice called *time blocking*. This is especially useful if you are desiring to start your own business while still holding a full-time job, or if you are seeking to upgrade your job. It requires that you set aside a block of time every day to pursue your new passions for the area you want to end up in. During this set time, eliminate all distractions, and focus on the important tasks that support your priorities. Do whatever is necessary to create a distraction-free environment—turn off your phone, close the door to your office, and put up a do not disturb sign to be twice as productive.

Time blocking is your friend. It's very easy to go through a day and find, at day's end, you've frittered it away in trivial matters. And you've lost a day in making inroads to creating your new future. I block chunks of time in my schedule, and sometimes set aside an entire day to focus on one thing.

How about trying this? Maybe once a week or even every day, block the time to spruce up your presence on social media, or update your resume on business platforms. Use the time to rebrand yourself and build a positive reputation, by posting articles on business platforms and programs to establish yourself as an authority in your chosen area. You can get a lot of free advertising, and build high-level influence this way.

Branding or rebranding yourself is always a smart move. It isn't just about dressing differently or getting a new haircut, although those come into play too. It's about identifying your strengths and skills, and bringing them to the forefront. You rebrand yourself to make it easy for prospective employers and clients to recognize your experience and what unique value you can add to their companies or their projects. Ask yourself what makes you special. Is your online presence in sync with who you are? Have you listed high-profile projects you may have worked on, or offered testimonials from happy clients? Check with a branding expert how to leverage these assets.

Have you updated any speaking engagements you've participated in, or workshops you've conducted? What about your professional memberships and alliances? Or online courses you may have enrolled in? Do the articles and comments you post reflect the full breadth and depth of your professional skills and knowledge? Don't underestimate your worth, and don't overlook any skill or experience that may give you an edge in the marketplace.

There are plenty of resources available where you can learn how to brand and rebrand yourself, as well as free webinars available at the tap of a key. Just don't get caught up in the upsell of what they then offer for more learning. Learn what you can from the free webinar, and move on to the next thing.

I suggest you build a free website with a domain that is in your name. You can set up a website with a free management system and blogging tool, which are readily available online. There are ready-made templates designed for every business. Having a website and an email with your domain name conveys an image of success. For example, my real estate email address is Nora@NoraEllen.com, which is more impressive than Nora@gmail.com.

Consider researching network marketing companies through which you can make money rather quickly. Mary Kay is one such beauty company many people know of, and there are numerous ones in the areas of health, like Juice Plus, in cleaning supplies, and more. It is helpful to an entrepreneur starting out these days, that you don't have to carry inventory, as you might have had to in the past. All you need is to make a small investment, even under $100, to become a distributor and to start selling products that you have benefitted from and believe in. It requires work to build a customer base and to sign up and nurture a team network under you, but it is something you can start on even while holding onto your current job or business.

Network marketing companies have developed their products and invested into building a solid marketing and training system, and if you put in the time to learn how to work these systems, you will make headway. The company will have support and a community for you to grow with. Amongst the various benefits, you learn how to operate a business, communicate with people, and build up residual and passive income.

I am not going into great detail about network marketing, but suffice to say, it is a good way to learn how to run a business and start making money without it being too costly for you. Just know that there is a difference between multi-level marketing companies and network marketing companies when you are doing your research. Focus on those companies that are successful and whose products or services you are interested in.

I hope I have sown some seeds to get you thinking about new directions and new possibilities. You don't have to do everything at once, but I encourage you to do at least one new thing every day. Give that one thing your full attention when you are carrying it out, and you'll find you become more productive than if you were juggling several things in the air. Not every new pursuit will work, but at least you can check it off your list if it fails to lead to anything. But most of all, remember, you are unique; there is no one else in the world like you, and you are worthy. Help is all around you. Be willing to ask for it.

Chapter 8

Awaken the Leader in You

"Don't follow the crowd; let the crowd follow you."
—Margaret Thatcher

One of the joys of hosting my podcast, *Women Starting Over*, is that I get to learn from incredible women from all around the world. I am privileged to share their success stories with my listeners, who may be seeking help or inspiration in finding their own way forward. In this chapter, I decided to include an episode I had with Councilmember Laura Kaino. I picked this particular episode because it was about how two women became leaders in their communities, which is one way to springboard into financial success.

Here is the fun transcript of the episode, with slight changes for readability.

Nora: This is going to be a very unusual podcast because it is about women in leadership positions, like elected officials or some kind of position that a woman has that gives her authority. I just love topics about women and leadership, and how women get there. I've been the vice mayor of my city, as an elected official. I was elected twice. I'm termed out because the city where I live has term limits, which means that after a certain time, you can't run again. You have to sit out for years or some time frame, depending on where you're from. I have asked my guest, who is also an elected official now, to be on this podcast episode to share her thoughts about women in leadership.

We are going to talk about how each of us ended up in the leadership positions that we did. This is like on the city level, a municipality, but we are voted in. Here in the United States of America, our cities have mayors. Not everyone knows that along with the mayor, there are also council members who are also elected. In the city that I live in, we are what we call "at large." We campaign to the entire population, which is about a quarter of a million people. There are other larger cities, say like Phoenix, where it's divided into districts; so you can only vote for the person running in your district, and because Phoenix has almost two million people, it's just divided more that way.

My guest is a wonderful council member from the city of Goodyear, which is a part of Phoenix. So both of us live in the Phoenix Valley. Welcome to Councilmember Laura Kaino.

Laura: Hi, Nora; thank you so much for having me on. I have to say that this is another first in a line of many firsts that I've been encountering, but I am looking forward to talking with you today about our journey and how it is interrelated. So this is going to be a lot of fun.

Nora: Right, it is. Both Laura and I have had different paths to becoming leaders in our community, our cities. I had served on my city council as the only woman for years. And when I first got elected, there was only one other woman on council, and then I ended up later serving with all men. I believe, on your council, you have both men and women. Is that true?

Laura: Yes, but we do have a majority of women. Our mayor and three council members are female, and because it's an odd number, we have three men.

Nora: Okay, so that's great. Kind of a difference there between my city and your city, and that's okay. Actually, the men on my council, they were all very respectful of me, and it was a really wonderful experience.

Let's start with your journey. What got you started to even thinking about running as an elected official, or as becoming a leader in your city and your community?

Laura: That's a great question, Nora. My career was working with the city of Phoenix, where I've had almost 17 years of municipal experience, being on the staff side. So I loved my work there. I did Human Resources, which is people and problems, and people with problems. It really brought that human side to working in government, and learning lots of skills and having a great deal of responsibility.

The majority of my career was spent in the Water Services Department, which is a very technical department. Through my time there, I learned a lot about water and wastewater, and things like that, which were very advantageous to me as I moved forward. My story is a little unusual because it wasn't necessarily something that I aspired to.

I was starting to look at retirement, and starting to think about what life would be like after I left my Monday through Friday job. And I had a friend of mine, a Christian friend of mine, who said, "You know, I think I see in your future that you'll be in an elected position." And I thought, "Well, that's really interesting." I couldn't imagine that this would be a possibility, but I considered it.

Well, you know, it's interesting that when there is a plan that is bigger than you are, and you don't even realize it, the message will be confirmed. And it was. I had other people, including my pastor, tell me the same thing. It got me thinking that maybe this was a possibility. Sometimes other people see something in you that you don't see yourself, and they speak into your life. And so I started thinking about that.

But my dilemma was that I had no idea what steps to take. What would be involved? What would I even do? And that was almost paralyzing at first. It's like, okay, people are calling out that they see this in me, that I'm going to move to this new level of government service. But I didn't know what to do or how to go about it.

Nora: Right, and it really is wonderful when people say things to us, and we need to be listening and not discount what people say to us. Because that is also my experience as far as people saying, "Nora, you should run for office." And sometimes it's out of the blue, and you're like, huh? I started keeping a journal of my friends that would say that to me when they said it. My journey in starting is a little different from Laura's, in that Laura worked for a city, and learned a lot about municipalities and how they work.

For me, what I started doing is getting involved as a volunteer in different ways. I've been like a lifetime volunteer about all kinds of things. And I was doing it to serve, for one reason. The other reason was my real estate business. I am a natural networker, but also, in order to get new clients, I needed to serve in some different ways.

That's what I started to do because of my expertise. I was invited—appointed, I should say—by the mayor, to the city's Neighborhood Advisory Committee. It was a committee of a few people. We were all volunteers appointed to look over the neighborhoods, to see how everything's looking in the neighborhoods. Are they safe places? Are they beautiful? Because a mayor, and even the city council, can't know everything about what's going on in the city.

Most cities and towns will have volunteer groups. There are commissions and there are boards that they have, to help bring advice, and to take over some of the city responsibilities, where it's just too much for the mayor, council, and also the staff of a city. And I think it's a beautiful thing.

Laura: That also gives citizens an opportunity to get involved and see how the city works. I know that we really value our citizens who serve on these boards and commissions, because they do real work.

Nora: They do absolutely real work. We went out into the neighborhoods, and we would also encourage neighborhoods to do certain things to beautify their neighborhoods. We would have a grant to beautify their neighborhoods.

It is work, and every commission is different. I was on the Airport Commission as an elected official; that took a different amount of time than when I was a volunteer on the Neighborhood Advisory Committee. And then the mayor also appointed me to the Four Corners Retail Committee, where there's a bunch of people from different industries. We got together to talk about the retail corners that were starting to become blighted. We just wanted to head that off—prevent rather than wait until it's too late for that change.

So, people started telling you to run for office. What did you start doing after that?

Laura: Well, like you, I am a networker also, and it turns out we have a mutual friend. And so she had said, "I know somebody who is a council member in Chandler. I'll give you her contact information and you two can meet up."

So I called you. You were so gracious and we met for dinner. We talked about your journey and what it takes to actually campaign and have to get yourself out there, get your name out there, get involved. I remember that was a very significant turning point for me.

That was the first time I ever met you. And even since then, you would send me encouraging notes, and then we would run into each other from time to time. You always asked about how things were going for me. You always stood steady as a resource for me, just to say how important it is when you're trying something new, or you're taking a step of faith out there, that there are people who are rooting for you and are willing to give you information to help you move forward.

I've told you before, Nora, but I just wanted to thank you for being that woman for me, because I didn't really know anybody who had done such a thing. Anyway, after I retired, I began to get involved in the city of Goodyear, and I went to the Citizens Academy, and then to the Police Citizen Academy and, you know, started to make connections. I was appointed to the Arts and

Culture Commission, where I served almost three years. Then I was the chairperson for that. And so I would make presentations in front of Council. Then I was appointed to the Citizens Water Conservation Committee, in which my water experience really did come in handy. That was a two-year assignment, and we made a lot of recommendations. I didn't serve in a leadership role in that one, but we did do presentations to Council.

But also during that time, I would go to city council meetings in person and sit there, and I would watch how the business of the city is conducted from this side—watching the mayor, how she interacts, and how she responds to the public.

You know, typically the public doesn't show up unless, maybe, somebody is getting an award or recognition, or they're not happy about something. I would watch the dynamics of the Council, and then, just for persistence, I began to interact more with the Council members and staff, and get to know people.

Nora: Yes, those are very wise words, with what you're saying, with what you did. Which is what I tell my listeners on our podcast, that you always want to ask questions.

Find out what you need to know that you don't know. Get around the people who are where you're wanting to go, which is what Laura did. She was so sweet, she reached out to me. That's what we appreciate about mutual friends. You could ask them, "Who do you know that is in this position that I would like to have, that might mentor me or give me some good ideas?"

Neither Laura nor I had a clue. Really, how do you even run for office? What's going on in cities where I can serve or help? It takes people. With life, it is all about people. She did the Citizens Academy, which was a way to interact more with some of the city's stakeholders, and learn about the city. There's so much to cities that people don't sometimes know. Well, what does a council member do for her city?

When I was running the second time to get on council and get re-elected, I did a video about what a councilmember does. What does a councilperson do? We take care of the water for this city, the police department, the fire department, your city streets, how the city develops, and your city parks. There's a lot of things that we do for the city.

It's very different from state government or the US government. City officials are what we call non-partisan, at least here in Arizona. I'm really not familiar with other states; we're neither Republican nor Democrat. It's not a thing like that when it comes to political parties. We do make policy, like maybe building codes or deciding what developments are going to be right for the city.

We have staff. We have a city manager. We have a lot of staff people. So it really is different from other levels of government.

Laura, I love how you attended meetings to try to get to know council members, and to see how the city works. Believe it or not, I did not do that. I did not. We're all different, right? I did not attend those council meetings. Now, I knew the mayor and councilmembers because I was serving in the city. I was a board member on the Chandler Chamber Board of Directors, which was a business chamber. I'm a businesswoman; I love business. That kind of network, to me, meant more. I was also on some non-profit boards, and then you just start getting to know different people.

For me, a big turning point was when I was at one of our Chamber Board luncheons. They seat the board members, kind of where they want. They put your little name placard, and you find it and you sit down. One time, I was seated next to the mayor. I already knew him; we knew each other, and we just started talking about an upcoming election.

There are times when there are people running for positions. They are qualified. They would be great at what the position requires. And there are some other people, and they may not know what the responsibility is; they may not be ready. They might have the heart to do it, but they might not be able to. That's how I'm going to put it, and sometimes there's people running that might be . . . they're just not ready. That's how I'm going to say it. Anyway, sometimes that happens. The mayor encouraged me to run, and I didn't take that seriously then.

I texted my son on the way home, "Well, I guess I'm going to run for the city council," as a joke. I was joking with him. But then the next day, I started getting phone calls. In fact, my son called me and said, "Hey, Mom, what's going on?" Because he was getting calls from councilmembers and different city stakeholders. And, Laura, I knew in that moment. Okay, the mayor, I call it, started a fire. That's how I thought. Okay, so then if he's behind me, wow, maybe I should do this. Yes, and maybe now is the right time.

Sometimes there isn't a good time. My daughter was going to get married; her wedding was coming up. When you run for office, a person has to get signatures to get on a ballot. I had six weeks to get over a thousand signatures.

Laura: Oh, my.

Nora: I'm going to my daughter's wedding, I'm in real estate, I'm single, I'm working. I'm so busy. Anyway, I just knew in that moment that it was time. I believe God will set you up in your life, or you might be doing something for one reason. Like everything I did as a city commissioner. It was not even in my mind to run for office or be on city council. We have great people who were already doing great. I'm just not even thinking about it, and the next thing I know, boom! It was like, suddenly, I am running for a political office. Overnight.

Laura: And now what?

Nora: Yes, now what? It's great to get a lot of wisdom. And now, I did what Laura did. I started making calls. What's really cool is, if you're someone who is a good leader, people will rally around you. They will support you. Do you want to talk about how that happened for you, Laura?

Laura: Oh, absolutely. Well, you know, it is interesting, especially when people are terming out and there are going to be vacancies in those positions. Mayor and Council, I mean; they're not trying to hand pick, but they're also trying to look for people who had been engaged, who demonstrated an interest and a commitment, and to encourage them in the process. In my case, there was a vacancy to fill.

Somebody was on her last term, and she stepped down to go run for an office at the state legislature. At that point, there was an application and an interview process to fill her seat. Because I had served, and because I'd been showing up and all those things. I think there were about twelve people who applied, and out of that, they interviewed four.

I was the only woman who they interviewed. It was a really interesting experience because they don't just call you up and say you got the job. Oh, no, because it's public business, they announce it at a council meeting.

So there were four of us sitting in the audience that night. I got to look around and see who also had applied. It was on the council agenda. I just remember that it was the last thing on the agenda. The mayor, you know, announces an agenda item, and she turns to one of the council members and says, "Do you have a motion to make?" He said, "Yes," and I thought, "Oh, my gosh, this is that moment." He said, "I make a motion that we accept Laura Kaino as interim council member."

It was just like, oh, my gosh, this is that moment, when those words that were given to me, that initially I did not believe, came to pass. I was appointed as a council member. I finished that term, which was for about a year, and then the next step was that I needed to run in an election to get elected, which brought up a whole new set of "oh, my gosh, how do you do this" kind of circumstances. So again, it was about reaching out to people I knew, and people that knew people.

That's pretty much how I found the people I worked with. I've got my close friends that said, "I don't know how to do this either, but I'll go with you on this journey." I had just finished a class at Leadership West. It's a year-long class. Leadership West is a West Phoenix Valley driven program where they look for emerging leaders. They teach you a whole bunch of things, and you network, and then you have to do a project.

My project ultimately was to run for an office, which I ended up doing. But I had a ton of support from all my Leadership West co-graduates, plus it's a huge network of alumni. It takes a village to do this. This is in no way a one-person show.

For example, just getting the signatures to qualify to be on the ballot is very daunting. That is a big, big process. Then you have to raise money. That was something that was very hard for me because signs cost money, and Facebook ads cost money. And yes, flyers—flyers are tremendously expensive. I think about that every time I'm getting one in the mail right now. Ooh, that costs a lot of money.

Nora: It's always nice, when it's not your time to run or you're done in politics, which I am, and you get these mailers—and phew, okay, it's not my turn! Because you're right. It does take a lot of guts, a lot of stamina. You learn new things to run for office; in raising money, you have to do that "ask." It can be humbling, but it's needed, and it's very important to do that.

What you shared about being involved, I've been involved in the city, too. There are people that just come out of the blue, who want to run for a position, without relationship. I have a hard time with that. We have a term for that. It's called "carpetbagger."

Laura: Oh, yes, that is true.

Nora: Someone will run for an office, or try to, without having served in the community first, without having relationships. They try to say, "I care about you and I want to serve." That is not the way to do it. I strongly discourage people from doing that. I did tell someone that, who just came out of the blue and wanted to run, and whom none of us had heard of. I tried to talk to them, to encourage them to first serve in the city. Let us get to know you.

The other thing, too, what the person wanted to accomplish, wasn't even what we do on a city council. It's not even our responsibility. We don't do things with education. We have no authority; that is the school boards. That's the Department of Education for a state. They thought they could come and change what's going on in schools. And so there's kind of some misunderstanding of the role.

If you have a leadership position that you have your eye on—and I'm talking to my listeners—know what their responsibilities are first before you try to go for that position.

Laura: I totally agree with that. You're right; people think that if you work for the city, then you've got some say in your local education. We try to support our school districts and partner with them and things, but we are not policymakers, nor do we have any budget impact on their decisions.

Nora: We don't. We do partner in a lot of ways, to support each other and work together. So that is something that people do need to know. Being a city councilmember is not quite as sexy as some of the political positions that people might be in.

One thing I want to share too, which was kind of a big "aha" moment, was when my son was in office. It doesn't always take a position with a title, where you can be helpful or influential or make a difference. I've seen, sometimes—let's just take a position—where there's a president of a group. They could have a deputy, chief deputy, or someone who might have more power, more wisdom, and more influence, but we don't hear about that person.

So, sometimes we assume it takes a title to have influence, and that's not exactly true. If running for office is not something somebody wants to stomach, there are other ways to serve and lead. The thing is, leaders are really servants. They are serving their constituents. They are serving the people who are under them in responsibility. I respect people—elected officials, people in government, politicians—who got there because they were serving people. Sometimes they're serving people, but the public doesn't know about it because it's not something they hear on the news.

Laura: That is very true. And in my case, I mean, as I was meeting people and networking and trying to raise money and things, people want to know why you're running. They want to know who you are and what's driving you. I would get support because people would find that my reasons for running were to benefit the community, and it wasn't self-driven. That makes a big impact because, just like you said, people will run for all kinds of reasons. A lot of it is to magnify themselves or get themselves into a political place; it's a step to a political career and things like that. But without relationship, without serving first, people want to know—who you are, what you've done, and what your vision is. They're pretty discerning. If it's all about you, they're not as inclined to support.

Nora: Right, and that is really true, especially if we can get with those people; what I've noticed about politics and elected officials. Because, first of all, you have to run a campaign, and there are actually people who run a heck of a really good campaign, even though they might not be as qualified as another person, who maybe isn't the best at campaigning. So, campaigning is like marketing.

And I know a lot of elected officials and politicians—whatever term you want to use. I sometimes say "elected official" because . . .

Laura: Right, it's not as divisive right now.

Nora: Just a little side note. This little bunny trail is that most of us elected officials are really good people trying to serve and help and make a difference. But we don't often make the news.

Sadly, the ones that make the news are the ones that maybe are scandalous or are problem people.

Okay, I don't know how else to describe it. They are corrupt and they're the ones that make the news. I'm just noticing now, here in the United States, is we're starting to have this mindset that all politicians are that way and that is not true. I know for my son, he has sacrificed himself to serve Arizona, to be a blessing and help our state to thrive and grow in the right way.

So does he make the news? Sometimes, yes, because he's had leadership positions. But I see first-hand, and there are other people in these positions, where they're good self-promoters and they're good campaigners, but they're not the best people to have in the position they got elected for. That is why we voters do struggle with this. Wow, who do I vote for? If I just look at this campaign ad or their website—who doesn't sound wonderful on their ads or their website? Then there's the attack ads, and we say, "Oh, we don't like those attack ads," but sadly, they work.

Laura: Yes, they're terrible.

Nora: They are terrible, and we say we don't like them, but that's what happens, because they work. What I tell people is talk to someone you know and trust, who might have an idea who is running for office, or "who is who" kind of thing. There will be somebody in your sphere of influence that maybe will have more of an insider view of things. It's not always what we are presented in the media; because, sometimes good news doesn't really sell.

I'm just going to do another bunny trail here. I had a reporter call me one time about a vote that I had, where I voted against a council pay raise.

And the way it works in my city is that we'll have an action item where we vote on something. If it passes, even if someone voted no, then at the next council meeting, it will come through on what we call a consent agenda. There are like a hundred items we vote on, probably at every council meeting, because there are just little things, like what's going to happen on a street corner. Everybody's in agreement that we have to fix that street corner, and items like that, so they are put on the consent agenda.

I had voted no on the pay raise, and when that came through on the consent agenda the next meeting, I was so focused on a development that I thought was wrong for the city, that I forgot to vote no for it on the consent agenda. And what happens with the consent agenda is what's recorded for a final vote. So now I am recorded as supporting the pay raise. And so the reporter called me about this. I was talking about it and then said, "How come you guys don't report on things that are really hurting people, like our children, like sex trafficking. That is so horrific. You're going to call me about my vote instead?" I knew what he was going to do. He did; he twisted the story about my vote. In fact, anyway, the title, which he wrote in quotes, was wrong. You know what he told me? People don't want to know about sex trafficking.

They don't want to know what's going on with children that are being trafficked, and it doesn't sell. That's the thing, and I understand; they are a profitable business. I'm not saying I understand, but that's how it is. As consumers, we have to be careful what news we consume. Okay, that was kind of a little bit of a bunny trail.

Laura: Absolutely, and that thing too; a lot of the city business is not glamorous. It's pretty mundane. I mean, it's lights and traffic and roads and construction projects, and things like that. It takes a lot of study. You get the information, probably several days in advance, and you get the documentation, and you read it and then you can ask questions of staff. It's interesting that because of public meeting laws, you just can't talk to everybody else on Council; you can maybe talk to one or two. Then you have to make your own decisions. And so it's a very interesting process. I have had two "no" votes so far, where I've been the sole "no" vote on things that have developments, that have come up to us, because I didn't think it was in the best interest of Goodyear. In a way, it was sort of freeing; it's like, "Okay, yup, I can vote against something. It's okay. Nobody's mad at me."

The fact is, we all need to have different opinions and ways of looking at things too. We don't need everybody to be thinking the same way.

Nora: No, we absolutely do not. That's why we have multiple councilmembers, plus the mayor.

Laura: Yes.

Nora: I want to go back to what you did to get into some leadership programs. It is important to understand about leading. What does that mean? It's a learning thing to do. No one is born a leader. We all develop into leaders, or not.

When I looked back at my life and thought about how I got here in leadership, one thing I thought about, which I never realized at the time, was that we went to church while growing up in my family. It was in the church setting where our youth would have some different positions of responsibility; you would plan events, or you would welcome people, or that kind of thing. And also in my church, I would help in the nursery, or I would teach Sunday school. I was a volunteer in our vacation Bible school. I did a lot of things in the church that actually helped me become a leader, because we were taught to serve, to care about people, to help the poor and the needy. That's what I was taught in church, to reach out to the lonely, and that also set me up for leadership.

We're just about to finish here. And so, Laura, be thinking about something you might want to share that we haven't covered. I want to bring up a book by John C. Maxwell. He's like the leader of leaders here in the United States. He wrote a book that caught my eye while I was in an airport, walking by one of those book stands, and it's called *How Successful People Lead: Taking Your Influence to the Next Level*[2]. And I thought, "Wow, what is that book?" Because, even though I was vice mayor, I still had more to learn. The book has five levels of leadership.

The first is position. It's a great place to visit, but you wouldn't want to live there, and that's where you actually have a position of leadership.

The second one is permission. It says you can't lead people until you like people. The third one is production. Making things happen separates real leaders from wannabes.

The fourth level is people development. Helping individual leaders grow extends your influence and impact. The fifth one—I love this, and this was new for me—is called *the pinnacle*. The highest leadership accomplishment is developing other leaders up to level four. It's a great book if you're looking for a book about

---

[2] Maxwell, John, C, How Successful People Lead: Taking Your Influence to the Next Level, May 21, 2013

leadership ... how to develop leadership. It's basically about mastering the ability to inspire and invest in people, because you have to build a team that produces not only results but also future leaders.

Is there anything you would like to share that is inspiring and motivating, Laura, before we finish this podcast of Women and Leadership?

Laura: Well, thank you again for this opportunity. It's been a lot of fun having this conversation with you, Nora. We've talked today about the journey of private citizens going on to an elected official position, which is big and beyond anything that we had ever done.

But I just want to share about the steps that are taken when you're going to go up to some type of new level. Regardless if it's going to be something in the public sphere or maybe in some other setting, you want to talk to people who have done such a thing. You want to look to see what the steps are, where you can begin to learn and to become involved, whether it's volunteer or paid. You have to just take a leap of faith sometimes, and say "I don't know if I can do this, but I'll give it a try."

Learn what you can, do what you can, and make sure you have people around you that will be honest with you and help you along your journey. Many of us women, we have different stages in our lives, and for me, when my regular career ended, I was deciding, "Well, what am I going to do?" Then I really had to take this seriously and actually put my feet to work—put actions to this possibility. And so, I just think it's applicable, no matter what it is, that next step that you're going to take.

Nora: That is wonderful. Very good summary of our conversation. And Laura is the sweetest person; I just want to tell our friend who is listening in: When she met with me, she treated me to dinner, which was really nice. I definitely adore her; I was in awe of her servant heart and how she loves people and how she really cares about people. That kind of person makes a good leader, and that's why Laura is where she's at. Thank you, Laura, for sharing.

Laura: Thank you, Nora, for having me.

www.WomenMovingUp.com

Success Story from Mary Ann S. Chavez to Nora Ellen

It is a privilege to write to you about the impact you have made in my life. I say we have been friends for over 25 years! Among the many ways you have inspired me, I have you listed as a Spiritual Mother in my Bible.

When you first coached me, you said, "If you do just one thing, please take this program called, *Life Management Systems*." I did, and I look back at how much I grew in my personal life.

Because of your encouragement and coaching, I am NEVER A GLASS HALF EMPTY! You are a true inspiration for both women and men. Not only did you help me 25 years ago but you continue to help me NOW. I have started a new business with your help to see myself in a better light.

You have taught me not to give up, and not to quit. If there are times when I do want to quit, I can fall back on your advice and timeless coaching. You have helped me to not be negative but be positive and to find the best of myself. To smile and laugh. Oh, and I have also learned that it is okay to be single!

I have learned that I am not a failure as a mom or a grandmother.

Love you always,
Mary Ann S. Chavez

Chapter 9

The 8 Characteristics of Success

"In the end, it is the quality and character, a leader's understanding of how to be, not how to do, that determines the performance, the results."
—Frances Hesselbein

There's a lot at stake here. It's the rest of your future that you are shaping, and at times you may find yourself exhausted, confused, and possibly dispirited. This is the time when you want to challenge yourself, if you want to live a new life. This is the moment you want to push the boundaries of what's possible. This is that point in time that you need to dig deep, because success isn't just a question of luck. When you really think about it, successful people tend to share key personal traits that help them stay on course and stay ahead. Looking through all that I have done that has brought me to this point, I identified eight personal characteristics that I had first seen on one of the 50 business success flashcards by T. Harv Ecker. These particular qualities resonated so deeply with me, I am sharing them with you here, with my own personal take and interpretation. Cultivate these traits purposefully, and make them a part of you and your life to flourish in this world.

Characteristic #1 – Bravery

This is the quality that prompts you to step forward despite your fear. It spurs you to take action in spite of your worries. A great example of bravery is a story of my daughter, Juel, who was diagnosed with lupus when she was just 19 years old and still in college. I told her faith in God, to heal, is what is needed, but faith does not feel strong. Faith is not a powerful and intense feeling, like other emotions; it can feel very subtle. In fact, this is the most profound definition of faith that I know of: *Faith is the substance of things hoped for, the evidence of things not seen* (Hebrews 11:1).

I told my daughter that when someone has faith, they keep believing that what they want and need will happen. A person with faith will just focus on believing and acting bravely.

Juel was brave and held on to her faith. She chose to be brave in going through college while living with a chronic illness and she finished and graduated with 2 degrees in just 5 years. I am so thankful that Juel has had a lot of healing and is now the mother of three precious daughters, Liana, Hazel and Brinley.

Fear and doubt are the biggest obstacles to healing and achieving success. I link bravery and courage to faith. To me, they can be one and the same, because faith doesn't acknowledge fear; it recognizes what it is and acts anyway with a quiet confidence.

Do you know that fear is actually an anticipation of an unknown pain in the future, and more often than not, fear exists only in our minds? One way to have courage is not to indulge in the "what if" game—what if you had done it another way, what if you had taken a different job, what if you had married someone else? The "what ifs" do nothing for you. They consume crucial mental, emotional, and spiritual energy, at a time when you need all your best strengths within you.

Don't be a worrier. Worry is having faith in fear. I think of myself as being a warrior, not a worrier. Warriors don't give up; they give their all. They know that their communities depend on them, so they step up to protect their people. I love being courageous; I love being fearless. Mind you, I don't always feel brave and feisty. But to me, being brave and courageous is having the capacity to act, in spite of how I feel.

I am not suggesting you pretend you have no fear. Feel the fear and face up to it; but embrace courage and go for it anyway. It takes courage to take the risk of stepping into the unknown; it takes the courage of a warrior. You are a warrior, so go for it.

Just remember, you have God-given gifts, talents, and experience that no one else has, and God has a plan for you. So wherever God has placed you, wear your bravery like a cloak, like an outer garment, and don't back down. I have a little plaque on my desk that says, "Never, Never, Never Give Up," and I often look at it when I need a pick-me-upper. One of my favorite verses to stop fear is: *God has not given us a spirit of fear, but of power, and of love and of a sound mind* (2 Timothy 1:7).

Characteristic #2 – An Upbeat Attitude

One of the most defining traits of successful people is having an upbeat attitude and outlook. People who are bound for great things understand that success is not a straight line. There will be bumps along the way, and at times you may feel you are regressing two steps for every three that bring you forward. But it is the way you view the world and your circumstances that lay the foundation for success. Having an upbeat attitude means you are focused on success, even in the face of disappointments. It means you are willing to keep an open mind and learn from every lesson and every person you come across. It means you learn from mistakes and make tweaks to refine your way forward, rather than letting failure get the better of you.

Notice that successful people don't fall back on phrases like, "It's just my luck," or "Wouldn't you know it." Instead, they recognize that what you attune your mindset to is precisely what's going to come your way. If you keep lamenting about missed opportunities, you'll be attracting even more missed chances. Understand that you are—even at this moment of reading this page—creating what you want, because what you are focused on expands.

If you persist in thinking negatively, and blaming others or the environment or bad timing for your lack of success, you are persistently dragging yourself down. A person who is upbeat sees a world filled with possibilities, not impossibilities. With that in mind, find ways to lift up your attitude, and foster your drive and your self-belief to tirelessly achieve your goals.

My way to keep me positive and focused on the prize is to have home decor and framed art with motivational, inspirational quotes positioned where I can see them often as I move around my day. One of my favorites is in my office and says, "Proceed as if success is inevitable." I absolutely love the message to keep on going no matter what, because my focus on success leads me to the desired result.

Another one is from the Book of Proverbs, and it says, *"She is clothed with dignity and strength, and she laughs without fear of the future,"* which hangs right above my desk in my office. Are you moving toward your future with joy and confidence and strength? Or are you instead replaying old stories in which you were the victim or you had failed because of a bad mistake? Those negative thoughts belong firmly in the past, and it's how you think and act in the present that matters. Choose to be surrounded by words and affirmations, and just as importantly, people who support your upbeat attitude. No one wants to hang around a person with a negative outlook on life.

Characteristic #3 – Integrity

I am not fond of lies, be it a little white lie or an outright, bald-faced lie. I know that sometimes people give into saying a white lie to make someone else feel better. But it doesn't help you at all in the long run. I treasure integrity and honesty most during those moments when no one is aware and no one is around to know if I am carrying out an act of dishonesty.

For example, if at the grocery store, the cashier undercharges me or gives me too much change, I could walk away and feel good about paying less or coming away on top. Instead, I will draw attention to the discrepancy. That's because I want to be true to myself, because it feels good when I am a person of integrity, and it feels good that other people know they can count on me to be honest. The best relationships are built on trust; without that element, nothing good comes out of it.

A person who is constantly lying or adding another act of deceit on top of another, is always going to worry about watching his or her back, about being found out, and being presented with a multi-million dollar lawsuit. The people who commit fraud do so because they impatiently want financial rewards now. They don't want to put in the work for it, so they set out to deceive those who are less skilled at catching their lies, or those who are more vulnerable and trusting. Lying, deception and dishonesty are just plain wrong and not to ever be minimized or dismissed. It is always a freeing feeling to have a clear conscience.

We all want people to be honest with us. There are different kinds of honesty: relationship honesty, business honesty, financial honesty, and honesty to speak truthfully and lovingly even in the most confrontational of situations.

Integrity is also a sign of self-belief. It is the mark of an authentic person who is fully comfortable in their own skin. When you believe in yourself, you don't have to lie and cheat to make yourself appear bigger, better, or more important than you are. No, when you are comfortable in your own skin, you are living the best version of your life, with your own brand of individuality, skills, talents, passions, and gifts. Not everyone will like you, but when you are authentic and true, it won't matter that you are not Ms. Popularity; you'll be supported by the people who truly matter.

Characteristic #4 – Trustworthiness

This characteristic kind of overlaps with honesty and integrity, but being trustworthy is more integral to relationships. When you sign a contract with someone, you have to prove that they can trust in you to carry out your obligations as promised in the contract. Trustworthiness implies that you deliver what you say. You don't overpromise just to get the contract, nor do you try to paper over the cracks because of failing to deliver what is expected of you.

Being trustworthy is one of the most important qualities in life. It's the foundation on which relationships are built. Because our societies are built such that we are designed to be in a relationship with others, being able to trust each other means that we can achieve more together and go further together. Being trustworthy means you do what you say you will do. Implied in this is that you set realistic targets to get a job done right the first time. However, there is another side to trustworthiness: You have grace under pressure. When you are wrong, you admit you are wrong and own up to it.

Even as we pride ourselves on being trustworthy, there are times when we are in the wrong. We all make mistakes. There is something wonderful about having the guts to apologize and ask for forgiveness, with the result that it will open doors. Please note: I am not talking about those circumstances in which someone deliberately committed a crime, or horribly hurt and abused another. I am referring to those situations when you intentionally or unintentionally say an unkind word or accidentally overlook someone's request for help.

During those instances, whether you intended to hurt the person or not, when you reach out in sincerity to ask if they would please forgive you, it tends to soften the heart of the other person. You are now in a better position to regain that person's trust and feel better yourself.

Use phrases like, "I need to do better next time," "I'll work on this for the next time," and genuinely apologize. Be sincere and don't leave out anything; be open and honest. And leave it to the other person to get back to you in their own time. Forgiveness is a gift you give yourself and the other person.

Trustworthiness runs both ways. You want people you can trust, but you need to be trustworthy too, to ensure the relationships run smoothly. Being humble is part of being trustworthy, as is the willingness to admit when you have done wrong and know you need other people in your life. All of us have experienced, to different degrees, some level of lack of trustworthiness or betrayal.

There is betrayal in marriage, in friendship, and in business, and no matter what label is put on it, betrayal in every instance hurts. And earning trust back, whether it's you who broke the bond or the other, is hard and takes time. If you find yourself having been let down many times in the past, you need to make some changes. One of them is to hang out with different types of people, because when you are capable of and sincere in wanting to support each other, you'll go further than if you had to do it alone. This reminds me of the famous *Golden Rule*, where the Lord Jesus Christ said to "do unto others as you would have them do unto you" in the Sermon on the Mount. Being trustworthy is a beautiful and crucial characteristic for success.

Characteristic #5 – Persistence

When I first started in real estate, I had to become persistent in getting my first client. One day, I said to myself, "I'm going to do an open house of a house for sale. I'm going to sit at the open house every single day until I get a client." There was an open house available, but it wasn't my listing. Nonetheless, my associate was kind enough to let me sit in on her listing, and I turned up every day determined to secure my first client.

Sure enough, 10 days later, that happened. A couple, newly moved to the Phoenix Valley, came to the open house. They were just looking around. We hit it off immediately, and I helped them find a beautiful home in a lovely neighborhood. After the sale, I knocked on every door to get to know the neighbors and to introduce myself as the realtor that successfully sold the home to the newest residents in their community. During each introduction, I mentioned that I was available to help them sell their home, when they chose to do so. I ended up selling 13 more houses just in that vicinity. My first client and my subsequent run of successful sales came from my dogged persistence. I was not going to give up.

I was also persistent in calling everyone I knew to let them know I was now selling real estate. It was uncomfortable at times, but it was what I needed to do to succeed. I made it a point to keep in touch with those who gave me permission to tell them about what's happening in the real estate market. This persistence led me to have loyal clients who gave me great referrals and helped me succeed financially.

When I first ran for political office, I had to get over 1,000 signatures of registered voters in my city in just 6 weeks in order to get my name on the ballot. My daughter was getting married at the time, which meant I would be away for part of that time. I went all out to get the signatures, and I was successful in turning in what I needed to get on the ballot. I worked hard in my campaign and won because I did not give up, even though I was running against 6 others, all of them men.

Persistence pays off. Greatly.

Characteristic #6 – A Mindset for Hard Work

Having a mentality of being hard working is linked to being a warrior. I was recently thinking about starting a new company. You hear from many entrepreneurs that starting a new business is a lot of hard work. But here's a question: What does "starting a company is hard work" mean if you've never ever created a business for yourself?

You're treading on new ground, you have to juggle a lot more balls in the air, and you're facing stresses that you've never encountered before. It can be too much, but here is the secret ingredient for success: old-fashioned hard work. When you have a mindset for hard work, you have what it takes to just press through what you need to do, no matter how much you dislike it.

Some people dislike details, and others dislike routine. For me, I like many things a lot better than getting a website set up. Just thinking about it is a little stressful for me. But I find ways to pump myself up and just get it done. That's what a hard-work mindset does for you: It gives you the discipline and the wherewithal to take on what is necessary, regardless of whether it is boring or difficult or unenjoyable.

Understand that there is a difference between hard work and productive work. Be mindful of this difference, especially when you get overwhelmed. For example, you may feel you need to go through all your emails, or immediately react to someone who texts you or sends you a direct message on social media. Before you routinely react to such notifications, ask yourself if getting hijacked by someone trying to get you to do something for them, is fruitful to your long-term goals. I'm not suggesting that you ignore people, nor am I saying that you don't provide a service that you're paid to do. Just make sure you're not avoiding the actual work that needs to be done to reach your goals.

We are lucky to be living in a time when we are so connected; we can communicate at the click of a button. But as society has evolved, with more and more channels of immediate communication—texts, instant chats, on screen conversations, pop up messages—it has changed people's expectations on how quickly they expect to be responded to.

You need to de-escalate such expectations from those people who insist on instant responses; otherwise, your valuable productive time and energy will be whittled away by someone else's agenda, not your own.

One thing I have learned is that doing something new, such as what you're doing in starting over, will feel like hard work. For someone else already experienced, it's no longer hard, but it was when they first started. New work you've never done before can feel like it is too hard, but this is the right kind of hard work needed to reach success. And you can do it.

Characteristic #7 – Maintain Vitality

I am noticing that more and more people are complaining of constant fatigue, and I think that is because we, in the United States, overburden ourselves with too many activities that sap our energy. Even mindless television watching and lack of exercise can sap our strength. We are overdoing and stuffing our days with activities, compared to cultures in Europe and Asia, where they build in time with friends and family into their days.

Safeguard your energy; you need it to get through this time of great change. Look through your daily activities, and take note of those bad routines and habits that eat into your energy. For example, what is your bedtime routine like? If you go to bed mulling over your problems, you're not going to wake up refreshed and ready for another new day. Instead, be grateful for your day, thank God for the successes you had, and enjoy restful sleep knowing you've done your best for that day.

Sure, there are problems to be solved and errands that need to be attended to. But put them on a list and nurture your emotional and mental states by congratulating yourself on what you've done right. Celebrate big and small successes.

Check into your nutrition. Are you drinking enough water to stay hydrated which gives you energy? I live in the Phoenix Metro Valley, where summer temperatures can be well above 100 degrees, and I take care to drink a lot of water. What about your food? If you're constantly tired, can you make one change in your diet to swap out processed food for a vegetable or fruit?

Start your day right with a morning routine that serves you. I've mentioned this before, and here's a little reminder. When you wake, express gratitude for the new opportunities that are going to turn up that day, because gratitude wires you for success. I journal in the mornings, and I have my goal lists. I am continually tweaking my morning routine to be more intentional in what I do during the day, rather than winging it like I used to. Create daily rituals that power you forward. Be mindful of the little things that you do every day that needlessly rob you of your time and energy, because those little routines define who you are and what you achieve. Pay attention, and make appropriate and beneficial changes.

Characteristic #8 – Be an Expert in at Least One Area

The more you focus on your area of expertise, the more experience you gain and the better you get, and the more people get to know about your reputation. When you establish yourself as an expert, people will seek you out. If you are seeking a promotion or raise, being an expert sets you aside from other colleagues. Becoming the best in at least one area of skills builds character.

It is often most profitable to be the best in one area. Right now, there is a multitude of ways to improve yourself in your area of expertise. There are countless webinars online, free videos on how to do it, books, podcasts, seminars, and conferences. Be willing to spend a little time bettering yourself (most people won't) so that you can spend the rest of your life living it on your terms (most people will fail to achieve this).

Once you become a recognized expert in your field, you will be able to command a premium, because customers will be willing to pay more for your expertise. Becoming an expert accelerates your career, maximizes options for you, and broadens the scope of your options and opportunities.

How do you identify what to be an expert in, if you have multiple interests and experience? What is the demand in the marketplace? Is there an area you enjoy more? To be an expert requires that you put in the discipline, the focus, and the time. You must genuinely and sincerely want to do the work to get to the expert level. With that being said, find something that you are truly good at and passionate about, because when your passion is set on fire, you'll be deterred by nothing.

Your enthusiasm for your passion will draw others to your expertise, and you'll be looked to and consulted by clients and media for your opinions. As an expert, you'll get invited into peer networks that you couldn't previously break into.

Experts are drawn to one another; they recognize the hard work that has gone into acquiring expertise, because they have gone through the paces themselves, and there is mutual respect. And just as importantly, experts are willing to recommend other experts to their clients, because they have the fullest confidence in their skills, and they know with certainty that they will not let them down.

One suggestion I have, if you are still struggling to define an area of expertise, is to think about becoming a thought leader. Experts never rest on their laurels; they are always looking ahead for new ways of doing things more efficiently, and new solutions to deal with old problems. You can establish yourself as a thought leader in your field in many ways: Start a blog or a podcast like I have; consider writing a short eBook; submit papers to a professional organization; or frequently post your thoughts and opinions on business media platforms. Be willing to take lots of little steps, do them well, and you'll be on your way to becoming a thought leader.

Here's a thought: have you ever wondered how many millionaires there are in the U.S.? As of the writing of this book, the answer is there are about 12 million millionaire households according to the Spectrum Group. Do you know what the definition of a millionaire actually means? It is someone who has a net worth of a million dollars which is what they own, minus what they owe. There are millions of millionaires in every state of the Union. Millionaires are made in every kind of economy. I am a myth buster, if you haven't figured this out already. And this may surprise you, but millionaires don't look the way you might think they do. These millionaires are living among you. Guess what I am going to say next? Why not you? Yes, you can join these millions of millionaires.

Wherever you decide to end up, opportunity is everywhere for those who are looking for it.

Here's a tip: Take this time to reflect on all that you've learned up to this point. I would like to leave you with this important thought: As you go through this time of great challenge, promise, and renewal, remember that you are not alone.

You don't walk alone, because God loves you. I love you. No matter how rough or easy the going is, remember to love yourself and those around you so you can live a life well loved. Love yourself. Be appreciative of those around you who love you. It will make you a whole lot happier and will carry you forward through this difficult season of starting over and moving up.

Chapter 10

Negotiate Your Monetary Worth and Promotion

"Ask, and it will be given to you; seek, and you will find; knock, and it will be opened to you."
—Matthew 7:7

Are you a woman busting your chops at work, yet don't get the recognition you deserve? Are you the first to take on new responsibilities, but that promotion just passes you by? Have you put your life on hold for your career, but you're stuck in a rut?

Are you bumping across a glass ceiling, or is there something else at play here? I say that women are not earning what they deserve because they are usually not asking for what they deserve. As a group, we women often find it hard to talk about money. We are raised in a world that frowns upon us asking, let alone demanding, for what we want. We are reluctant to ask for something for ourselves, for fear that we will come across as being too pushy. We tend to think of others first, rather than ourselves. If that describes you, it is no surprise. You are reluctant to initiate such a conversation with your bosses, for fear that you may come across as being entitled, avaricious, called a bitch or too big for your boots.

The statistics support my point. A study by Robert Half[3], on the wage gap in the US, reports that 66% of women surveyed did not ask for promotions or raises; for men, it was only 54%. What does this mean? Simply that you need to learn how to own your value. There should be no shame or guilt in asking for a raise when you deserve one. It is time to shake off any fear or doubt you have about yourself. Stop sending out low-confidence signals to the decision-makers in your company, which may suggest you don't deserve a promotion.

Don't spend weeks overthinking or agonizing over asking for what you want. Turn a deaf ear to what your colleagues may say about you, and stop overanalyzing about asking for a promotion. Be firm, be confident, and realize that this is all about doing business, nothing more.

If you are uncomfortable about negotiating for a raise or a promotion, the only one who suffers is you. Stop leaving money on the table. Understand the culture of the company you are in; map out a trajectory for your career path within the firm, and ask your bosses if that is workable. If they say no, you might want to look elsewhere for another job.

There are times when you are awarded a promotion without a raise, or you get a salary increase without a promotion in status. My feeling is that it's better to get a promotion first, and

---

3 Starting Salary: Negotiable or Not? http://rh-us.mediaroom.com/2018-02-05-Starting-Salary-Negotiable-or-Not Feb. 5, 2018

then ask for a raise later—should you decide to negotiate for a job elsewhere, you are coming from a perceived position of strength.

What If You Were Overlooked

The loss will sting, and it might even feel humiliating, especially if your colleagues knew you were aiming for the promotion.

You may think you've failed, but know this to be true: There is an upside to failure. One is that it helps you clarify what you really want and whether you can meet the demands of a higher-level job. The other is that it forces you to sit down and fully evaluate what your strengths and weaknesses are. Use this time to identify where you may not have fully shown your abilities, and evaluate what you need to do to rectify the weaknesses. Were you waiting for something to come to you, instead of going out and asking for it? The third is that the setback may push you to make a career-altering pivot you maybe should've made a long time ago.

Ask to speak to your boss or the decision makers to gain some insights on why you were not considered, and what you can do to make sure you are in the running for the future. Prepare a list of questions that helps you gain insight on the factors that shape the decision-making process in your company. Be gracious with the answers that you get from your boss and don't bristle at any perceived negative comments. This is a time to gather important information you may have missed. Also, be willing to show that you have evaluated your own situation and are ready to rectify the gaps in your skills.

If you are anxious about doing this, set yourself a deadline to set up a meeting, and have someone hold you accountable so you don't let this fall between the cracks. If you are concerned or afraid to do this, here's how to put a positive spin on your anxiety: Fear is not always a sign you are doing something wrong; it is a sign you're about to do something courageous. So go for it! And plan a pleasurable reward for yourself when you do.

Do Your Homework: You need to set the stage right before you step into your manager's office to ask for more money or a promotion. You need to identify the right time, boost your own confidence, and make a powerful case for yourself, with facts and figures. You have to anticipate all the reasons your boss may say "no" to your ask, and be ready to explain what you bring to the table that warrants a pay raise. Also, be prepared to address all these issues with your boss, logically and unemotionally.

Identify the Right Time: Ask for a face-to-face meeting; don't settle for a text, email, or even a phone conversation. Be strategic about when to approach your boss to have a meeting. Mornings are usually better, as everyone is fresh and has time to chat. Never ask to meet on a Friday or a Monday; I suggest Thursday as an ideal day because that gives the decision-makers an extra day should they want to settle the matter before the weekend. Have at hand a good explanation should your boss (or the boss's assistant) ask for the nature of your request. Suggest that you would like some help with some work issues, or subtly mention that it is related to your performance.

Be aware of what's happening in the firm. Asking for a raise when the company is in the midst of big budget cuts, or facing financial strain, is not necessarily a good idea. The more appropriate times to bring up the topic are:

- During your performance review.
- After you've made a critical contribution to your department.
- On completion of a big project in which you achieved a crucial milestone.

Build a Strong Case: You want this to be a positive win-win meeting for everyone, so come prepared with metrics, ideas, and suggestions. Plan this out and, if necessary, work with a mentor or a coach to build the strongest case possible. Do everything you can to avoid going into the meeting blind. This is the time to show what you are worth, and the more prepared you are, the better your case and the more convincing you are.

Come with a specific figure, and do your homework so as not to lowball yourself. Do research in the marketplace. Check out reputable salary information websites to strengthen your understanding of your worth in the marketplace. Find out what your peers are earning for your level of education, training, experience, responsibilities, achievements, and extra certifications. Also, research earnings for the size and type of company you work for. Don't just focus on the salary figure; look at the perks and privileges as well, such as bonuses, benefits, vacation days, transportation allowances, and severance payments that are fitting for the kind of position that you want. And while I suggest raising a specific salary figure with your boss, internally establish a range that would reflect the highest level you are shooting for, and the lowest salary that you would be okay with. I call it BAN: know your Bottom Acceptable Number.

Check to see if there is a gender wage gap that exists within the industry and within your firm. If your boss is a man, argue your case like a male colleague would, but within your feminine qualities.

Bear in mind that even if your boss agrees with you, he or she may have to sell your case to their superiors, so give them all the ammo they need. Come with recommendations from clients, and positive emails from team members who have worked with you, and have on hand any endorsements from sponsors or mentors who will speak up for you.

In asking for a promotion, be willing to share in detail how an expanded role for you will generate positives for the company, be it in new revenue generation, cost cutting, or team motivation and dynamics. Stress your leadership skills to show that you know your stuff.

The Day of the Meeting

You've done your homework, and you have metrics to strengthen your case. But there are just a few more things to take care of before you walk into the meeting. Take care about your appearance: Don't turn up in sweatpants and a t-shirt, no matter how casual the company dress code may be. Dress like you mean business.

Look the Role You Want: Be presentable and be fresh. If you have to, get a new outfit, a new hairdo, or even a beauty treatment to boost your sense of self-confidence. Look and speak the part that you are rooting for. Practice what you want to say, with a friend, or video yourself to look out for giveaway facial tells, unflattering body language, and verbal garbage such as "um, like, you know." Check if you are speaking too softly or too loudly. Are you talking in a tone that invites conversation? Do you have an upbeat attitude?

Prepare your ask in advance, and identify the key words you need to say. Don't wait until the meeting to formulate your thoughts. Instead, practice your promotion pitch with a friend or even a coach, who will bring up the tough questions you may be asked.

You will likely be anxious before you step into the meeting, so do whatever you need to do in order to elevate your mood. As previously mentioned, one thing I do to get into a more positive frame of mind is to say "YES, YES, YES!" out loud in rapid succession, until I feel my body chemistry and posture change right before going into an appointment.

How to Present Yourself: When you are in your meeting, speak politely and with confidence. Leave the resentment and pride at home. Don't start with a complaint about how you've been overlooked, nor your dissatisfaction with why you are not getting paid enough. Consider the point of view of the person before you, and tailor your pitch accordingly.

Mention your value, and describe clearly what sets you apart from your peers without criticizing them. Draw out a time line of your responsibilities, from the time you started to where you are now, and the extra work you have taken on your shoulders. Stress that you are happy with your current responsibilities but are willing and able to take on more.

Talk about accomplishments you have achieved that have benefitted the company, such as realizing savings and streamlining work processes. Present documents, data to support achievements including revenues gained, new clients signed and what they are worth, and new projects started. Talk about your role as a leader and how you may have impacted your department, and how your leadership qualities have helped the company move toward its major goals.

Be ready with answers to questions that your boss will likely ask. When answering, be polite but also be clear and present your ideas as if you are talking to a team member, rather than a superior. Show gratitude and say thank you to suggestions that may be given to you. Use terms that invite collaboration, such as, "I understand your concerns," "Would it be appropriate if we could discuss . . . ?" When you feel the timing is right, confidently present your case as to why you should be getting paid more. You may want to come prepared with a notepad to jot down some quick notes to remember about the conversation. You could also have some points written down you want to be sure to cover, including your BAN. Maybe put a tiny smiley face or star to congratulate yourself on being there. This may sound funny, but it can give you a boost of confidence.

In closing a meeting, it may be appropriate to give a boss a summary of what you wanted to discuss for them to refer back to. If necessary, follow up with an email expressing gratitude for their time and summarizing your conversation.

Prepare for a No: Know that you'll possibly be told "no" on your first ask. There are several reasons this may happen, and it doesn't mean you didn't do a good enough job. Don't shut down when that happens. Instead, listen carefully to what your boss is saying, as it contains valuable information for your career path. Alternatively, your boss may be testing your seriousness and your commitment to the company. If a "no" blows you off, then you are clearly lacking in commitment. Your boss might say, "We just don't have the budget now, but we still want you to stay as we appreciate your hard work." Use that as a jumping off point to discuss the company's expectations of you; ask as to when it would be right to check back, and prepare an action plan to ask again in the next cycle.

Recognize that a promotion doesn't just affect you. It impacts the entire company as a whole, and you may get a "no" because there are important deadlines that will be impacted by your promotion. If you look at it from your boss's point of view, you may understand the need to time your move up in such a way to generate the least disruption within the department and the company.

Getting a no isn't the end of the world. Instead, view it as the beginning of a useful conversation, and be proud of yourself for asking. And the good thing is that your company is now aware of your desire for these kinds of changes.

Prepare for a Yes: When you do get a yes, don't act surprised. Show gratitude and ask questions to clarify your new role and your new job description, and when your raise will begin. Understand the new lines of reporting and who your new team members might be. If this is not the right time to go into such details, secure a next meeting before you leave the room. If appropriate, follow up with a short email expressing gratitude for their time and appreciation in anticipation for your new role.

Leverage an Outside Offer: Using an outside offer to get a raise is a legitimate way to get more money. But how you handle this is crucial to your future in your current firm, and there are downsides if you mismanage it. But first, the positives. Having an outside offer gives you confidence; it gives you information about other companies' compensation standards, and it strengthens your case to ask for a raise.

Now for the negatives. Your boss may not counteroffer but ends up wishing you good luck instead; and just like that, you have no choice but to accept the other offer. Another risk is that you may be seen as being disloyal, so don't come in threatening to quit.

If you are inclined to staying within your current firm, bring up the external offer by saying that you've been "receiving a lot of calls from head hunters, but I'm not interested." You can also say, "I plan to stay; please level with me as to my future prospects here." Or if you have a serious offer in hand, present the offer as a chance for your boss and you to "problem-solve" together on how to come up with a win-win solution.

Present your point of view as to why you seriously considered the offer, and present alternatives for the company to offer. Understand that your boss may not be able to match the money but is in a position to give you better assignments, enhanced training, or even alternative work arrangements, like working part-time from home. Don't get overly caught up with the salary number; instead, find ways that you can enhance your career path, because that will more greatly impact your lifetime earnings.

Negotiating the Best Terms on a Job Offer

The optimal time to negotiate the best terms for yourself is when you are first offered a job. This is the time to be upfront and firm about what you want, as 80% of employers expect you to ask. It demonstrates initiative, and stresses that you know your own self-worth. Don't make salary expectations the first thing on your list, as it conveys the image that money is all that you care about and there may be other benefits just as rewarding.

When presented with an offer, look at the details, and wait. Most people are uncomfortable with silence, so let the prospective employer fill in the gap. Remember, your employer has most likely taken months to find you. Take your time; don't immediately accept or reject an offer without getting all the relevant pieces of information. Ask away: Do they have a sign-on bonus? Who do you report to? What is your job title? Are there incentives, like relocation allowances, flex work hours, childcare, vacation days and time off, and on-site and off-site training? What is the likely path for promotion?

At every step of any negotiation, be prepared to walk away. If the company refuses your asking salary, leave the door open for further discussions down the line by asking what the likelihood is for a pay raise within the next several months. The answer will clue you in as to what you can fully expect.

Lastly, ensure that everything discussed is put in writing. Don't rely on just a verbal discussion, as it leaves too much room for misperception and miscommunication. If you receive the new terms in an email, respond through an email and make sure you save the email in both digital and print form. High level and executive positions are almost always presented in writing with the terms of the offer, and are typically in a formal letter. If you are offered a position in a phone call, feel free to ask if they would follow up in an email with the details of the offer.

You can take it one step further by putting the terms down on paper, in the form of a thank-you note. Write that you are grateful for the opportunity, that you are happy with the conditions of employment, and are happy to accept the offer.

Some Tips to Negotiate New Contracts with New Clients

First impressions are very important, so know your market. Be authentic and genuine to get the relationship off on the right foot. A sincere and positive attitude is the most important asset you can have at a negotiation, as these are the people you intend to work with over the long term.

Take your time; don't rush to sign on the dotted line. Most people dislike negotiating, and just want to get it over and done with. But contracts that are signed in a rush tend to be unworkable for both parties further down the line. Be reasonable, and do your research about what is standard in the industry, or consult with experts in the industry. Nonetheless, don't forget your end game. What do you really want? What are you willing to give in return for a concession? Believe in your worth for your expertise and realize women tend to underprice what they deserve to charge. Determine your fees from the place of confidence and market value, instead of fear and insecurity.

When negotiating my fees with a prospective client, at the point that they push for a discount, I demur and present my point of view. Here are a couple of lines of argument I use. I ask them that if I willingly gave away some of my own money by giving them a discount, would I not give away theirs later? If I easily gave away a discount, would this not reflect a lack of confidence in the quality of my work? Then I counter by saying that I offer more value than someone else who would be willing to charge less. You don't want to come across like you don't have enough work or are desperate. You could consider throwing in an incentive, like an add-on item, to add more perceived value, but hold the price at your desired level. Know your worth, and know when to walk away, as I have, from being underpaid, and from potentially difficult clients.

There are many ways to negotiate with new clients, depending on your area of expertise. I highly recommend enrolling in classes and courses on how to negotiate to build win-win outcomes for your clients and for yourself which help to build long lasting relationships.

Be mindful of what you can afford and are willing to handle, especially if you are at the start of a career and are in a rush to find new clients. Under certain conditions, you might be able to leverage a request for a discount to getting more business or getting a client to commit to longer terms. What you can offer will depend on the industry you are in, but here are some ways to agree to discount while changing the terms:

- Get the client to order more.
- Lengthen the time period of the contract.
- Take a secondary service/product out of the contract.
- Increase the order size.

New to the Workforce

There are a number of steps you can take to strengthen your position. Put together a compelling resume. No matter how qualified you are, the right resume gets you in the door for an interview. It creates the first impression on your prospective employer, and it presents snapshots of your important achievements in your academic and professional life. If you do not have much previous work history, be sure to include any volunteering or charity work you have been involved in. There are a surplus of online resources on how to craft the perfect resume and how to practice being in an interview.

When I decided it was time to get back into the workforce, I hired a career coach to help me make that transition. It turned out to be money well invested. If you can't afford this, track down online resources, access community events such as free workshops in the library, and check out guidance from women's organizations that are set up to help new entrants into the workplace. Or simply ask a friend who can help.

Use free templates online to prepare a couple of different resumes, to tailor it to a specific job. For example, an editing job in a publishing firm requires a different set of competencies from that of being a journalist, even though both of them are in the communications field. Even if a job may carry the same title, the shape of the responsibilities and the required skills and experience will vary from firm to firm. There really isn't a one-size-fits-all when it comes to preparing a resume.

You may need more than one kind of resume, as a resume needs to be geared toward the job you are applying for. Research the company you are sending your resume to, or the one with which you are having an interview, and ensure that you match the resume with the job. By taking this extra step, it shows you're up to the task.

And, remember. Everything you need is on the other side of a relationship. There are people ready to help just waiting for you to reach out and ask. This is your time to shine.

Chapter 11

You Are the CEO of Your Life

"You are the CEO of your life. You are in control of your future. So, do something great."
—Sharon Lechter

You're the boss, the president, the CEO. When I first heard this quote by Sharon, I felt a jolt of excitement. Understanding that I was the CEO of my own life, and that I held the reins to my own future, made me feel that everything was possible—because I was now in control of my own trajectory of success. Not anyone else. Just me. Whether you are an entrepreneur or working for someone else, you're still the boss of your own life. I hope these statements are exciting to you, because it means that you, and only you, get to choose how you want to be successful.

This is an exciting juncture in your life when you understand that you get to write your own ticket for success. Whichever way you choose to do it—starting your own business or working for someone else and moving up the ladder—doesn't matter. But I will say that the working world is undergoing massive changes.

Remote work or working from home is increasingly becoming the norm. The cradle-to-grave work ethic is quickly disappearing, and there's almost no such thing as a permanent job.

You've heard it countless times, but here it is again. Increasing digitization, because of fast and ongoing changes in technology, has changed the world. A search for meaning and purpose in work has changed the world. Being able to connect across thousands of miles, seamlessly, has changed the world. The rapid exchange of information, and explosion of ideas, has fostered an environment where there are innumerable opportunities to create new business possibilities.

But you may prefer the security of working for a company. If that is what you desire, then adopt these ideas to fast-track your way up in the corporate world. I don't plan to live off of just social security by the time I get older, and I wonder if it's even going to be available when I need it. I have not wanted to use my blood, sweat, tears, and time and energy for someone else, but just for myself. There are seasons in a person's life when starting your own business is a challenge—e.g., if you are a single mother. But there are many successful "mompreneurs" or single moms. One such person that I really admire is Mary Kay Ash, who I mentioned earlier, had defied the odds, because she believed in God, family, and business as priorities. She created an empire that is still strong today with this legacy that has outlasted her lifetime.

In my mind, the American Dream has changed; it's no longer just a nice home with a white picket fence. Now the dream is to be your own boss, become an entrepreneur and to run your own business. So why not have it all?

What are Legacy Entrepreneurs?

What is a legacy entrepreneur? I see the entrepreneur and business owner as a problem solver for other people. You can solve an existing problem or you can tweak an existing service or product to make life easier for your customers. It can be as simple as improving on the utility of a mop. Joy Mangano did precisely that. She invented the self-wringing mop, called it the Miracle Mop, and became a multi-millionaire. Although she is best known for creating the Miracle Mop, she holds more than 100 patents for her inventions.

What about Betty Nesmith Graham, who invented the correction fluid, Liquid Paper, which became better known as "white-out?" She was a secretary and artist, and a single mother, who became frustrated with making typos on her typing that she couldn't fix. So, she drew on her artistic skills and came up with a fast-drying, white tempera fluid and a correction brush. In the beginning, she and her son, Michael Nesmith, who later became a producer and musician in the group "The Monkees," would fill the nail-polish size bottles and slap on a label at home. She would later sell her company to Gillette, in 1979, for $47.5 million.

There are always gaps in the marketplace that you can fill. It's these gaps in the marketplace that you can fill or improve again and again, starting right now. Investing your time and energy and creating your own business is one of the most lucrative ways to amass great wealth.

You may be asking yourself right now, what service or product can you offer that isn't already in the marketplace? Keep your mind open and alert. Become an opportunist. Think about those times in your own life when you said, "I wish this object, service or product existed or was better designed."

I like to refer back to the exercise I suggested in Chapter 2, where I encourage you to "take an inventory of who you are and create a success list of your experiences, expertise, skills, gifts, talents, leadership positions, volunteer history, awards, recognitions, and successes."

Just the act of writing down the traits that make you unique, should help you come up with some ideas for a product, service, or information to sell that is differentiated from that of competitive offerings in the market.

As I mentioned, some of the best learning is "caught," not "taught." I am fortunate to have had an entrepreneurial dad who had his own real estate firm; he developed properties and had various investments. Not surprisingly, I became a successful real estate investor and broker along the way. But don't feel that you cannot be a business owner if you haven't "caught" the wisdom or grew up with entrepreneurial parents. Becoming an entrepreneur is really about having the right mindset. It is a mindset that requires you to understand that to leverage the skills and gifts for yourself, to rise above mediocrity and be the best you can, you have to be prepared to be really, really uncomfortable in the beginning, in order to be really, really successful all the way to the end.

Becoming an Entrepreneur

This is the time to be very organized with your time, your little tasks, chores, and responsibilities. Try cataloguing your time, and you may be surprised to see how much of it is frittered away by watching TV, playing electronic games, texting and chatting on the phone, and catching up with social media. As you add something into your life, you need to take something away.

If you have an idea to start a company, don't talk to naysayers and those who are broke. Talk instead to successful business owners, and study what they are doing right.

Revise old musty attitudes about selling. Some of the highest-paying jobs around are linked to selling something. Look at selling this way: You yourself have bought many things you wanted or needed from people and companies, and at times needed and asked a sales rep to help you make an informed decision. Selling is an important service that everyone needs.

In your own business, you have to be your best advocate in selling. You need to pitch your ideas to possible investors and new clients. You will be constantly marketing your idea, even in the face of initial disbelief. You have to be promoting yourself and that your new service or product has what no one else can offer.

Don't get caught up with elegant strategies and in-depth business plans. Sure, you need to do some homework to establish if your service is unique, and to attempt to identify your target markets. But don't get so mired in the research that you never get started. Robert Herjavec, who was one of the investors on Shark Tank and Dragon's Den, is known to have said on television that he did not do a business plan; he just started looking for customers to buy his (tech) product. He sold his tech company, BRAK Systems, to AT&T for more than $30 million, in 2000.

I thought it interesting that universities are now discovering that while it was easy to teach their students how to come up with business plans, ideas, and strategies, the students would get stuck in the execution. I believe this is because being able to successfully carry out detailed plans requires more than just nailing down the concept. You may be a visionary, and you come up with an idea for a blockbuster product. But if you cannot figure out the nuts and bolts of execution, or if your money thermostat is limited, your idea is only as good as it is on paper. If you cannot deliver what you promise, your vision remains just that . . . a vision. Ask yourself what you need in order to execute effectively in a start-up environment. Have you given thought to what may be subconsciously sabotaging you? Are your self-limiting beliefs and fears still at work in your subconscious? Are there embedded negative attitudes you may need to revisit and revise?

Make sure you do ample due diligence before starting. What kind of corporate entity is best for you? Do you need a partnership, or a limited liability company? Funding is often a big issue for new entrepreneurs. Every business has different financing requirements, and there is no one-size-fits-all.

Not sure where to find financial support? Look to readily available resources such as the US Small Business Administration, for information and tools. The SBA, for example, can offer an SBA-guaranteed loan, in which they step in to guarantee your loan if your bank thinks your loan is too risky. Consider also tapping into your own savings, borrowing from friends and family, raising money through online crowdfunding platforms, or approaching venture capitalists and angel investors. But, do this with a well thought out plan of how to pay the loans back. Everything should be in writing, even with family and friends.

Need some good ideas to start? A great way to process through what you have to offer and where you may want to focus is by using my free resource you can download to help you. Just go to my website, www.WomenMovingUp.com, and download to print the form titled "Your Business Arena Focus."

This is like a simple mind map that will assist you to:

- Pinpoint the various business product, services or information you have to offer.
- Nail down your target market.
- Prioritize your top three goals.

Too often, when you are starting off fresh, you can feel overwhelmed. This chart helps you narrow down what matters most to you, and gives you direction on where to go and how to start.

It's a diagram and worksheet to help you classify your skills into various categories and get specific in what you can offer in your particular area of expertise. It's similar to what a financial planner would do to help you devise a financial plan that includes a variety of stocks, bonds, college savings, retirement savings, etc.

When you use this tool, you list your top three goals in the top rectangle—what you have to offer and what you want to achieve. You'll list, in the bottom rectangle, the types of people, groups, and demographics that will need your specific services, product and skills. It's a method to help you focus, gain clarity, and plan your next steps forward. Then hang the diagram in your office to help focus and process through your arena.

Successful entrepreneurs have to take care of many aspects, one of them being building innovative systems that are replicable. McDonald's is so successful because it uses technology to allow its workers to speedily assemble replicable products. Their ingredients are the same around the world; they are stored and prepared in similar freezers and refrigerators in every store. The more replicable and systematized your business is, the easier it is to monetize, the bigger it will be and the wealthier you will be.

I believe that much of the work culture is moving toward consultants and contract workers, rather than full-time employees. If you're now working but would like to start your own business, you don't have to immediately abandon your day job. Consider first having a couple of clients and take small steps to start with. You don't need to be a full-grown company to have one or two clients; and when you have enough clients, you can leave your salaried job.

Have the right goals; if you are a fire-starter but are not good at following through, consider partnering with someone who has the ability to execute. Make sure you have a good team around you. You can't be an expert in every area of business, and you can't do it all by yourself. You'll need a team—such as a lawyer, an accountant, a manager, an illustrator, a graphic designer, a social media manager, or a product manager—depending on your type of business. You may not have the full team right away, but you have to decide how much you are worth and when you need to delegate tasks. I have had a housekeeper for many years. I know that the time I would have spent cleaning, I could use to make more money. Are you trying to save money in ways that actually amount to you losing out on opportunity, prospects, and therefore money?

Focus on where you want to end up. You're going to need a lot of faith, hope, and love. Surround yourself with those positive people who will give you the support you need.

Enjoy the challenge, and do it for the joy. I've previously mentioned that happiness is fleeting, and it is not my goal, nor is it my measuring stick of success. Joy is a steady flowing river that is the foundation of my being because of my personal relationship with Jesus Christ. There are times when I don't have the passion for what I am doing. I dislike routine, and having to do the same thing over and over again can be taxing. But I keep up with it because it's necessary in order for me to move on to the next step to success. I don't avoid it; I continue by reframing my mindset and seeing it as a necessary challenge, rather than as pain or annoyance.

Ultimately, everything comes back to people. Whatever you do, don't do it just for the money. When you can base your business on people and purpose, the profits and success will come. You'll be able to attract like-minded people who can partner with you and join with you, and you'll be helping people who need what your business has to offer.

Money is neutral, money is energy, and it is simply a tool. I've heard it said that the real purpose for money is to show appreciation, which is a beautiful thing. Money is something we trade for a service, product, or information. As people appreciate what you have to offer, the money will come. When you successfully serve those you come in contact with, you'll be assured of long-term success.

Remember, you are the only person responsible for your success. The exciting thing is that you can be as successful as you truly want to be, because you are the boss of your own life. You are more equipped now than ever before and this is your time to start over and move up on your own terms. Get going; think big, trust your instincts, have faith in God's plans and believe that you can do it.

www.ingramcontent.com/pod-product-compliance
Lightning Source LLC
Chambersburg PA
CBHW071401210526
45465CB00001B/202